"Sr. Kathleen Glavich's book, *Saints for Children*, is a wonderful, comprehensive resource about the lives of the saints. The variety of activities will be applicable to many different ages and interests of children. This book is a real treasure, a resource that will be used and enjoyed over and over."

Gayle Schreiber,
Author, *Saints Alive: Stories and Activities for Young Children*

"In *Saints for Children: Stories, Activities, Prayer Services*, Sr. Kathleen Glavich has come up with another blockbuster teaching aid. Using her typical creative, thorough, and practical style, she places at the teacher's fingertips everything necessary to present a well-developed lesson on the saints: comprehensive background material, thought-provoking questions, unique ideas for Christian response, challenging hands-on activities—and this results in making teaching and learning fun! The lives of the saints are presented in a straight-forward, inviting way and the discussion starters help children make connections with their own day-to-day struggles. Most importantly, the 'Things to Do' section, playlets, and crafts are sure to actively engage students in learning. Glavich's *Saints for Children: Stories, Activities, Prayer Services* is a definite 'must have!' Don't start the school year without it!"

Carole MacClennan
Author, *Learning By Doing*

"The appeal of Sr. Glavich's book, *Saints for Children: Stories, Activities, Prayer Services* lies in its challenge to the imaginative parent or teacher. While Glavich offers a repeated number of guiding suggestions, the brevity and directness of some suggestions leave open the way for the user of the book to make situation adaptations and to add other creative material built on the supplied directives."

Sister Mary Terese Donze, ASC
Author, *In My Heart Room*

"More than ever, our children need heroes and models to emulate; people who have lived the values and demonstrated the life-style we would like to see them begin to imitate. In this book, our children find the history of 12 such models, people who by the remarkable way they lived have earned the title 'saint.'

"A teacher or catechist need not adapt the language of this book for children—the author has used a clear, narrative style to tell the story of the saints. There is a saint for every month, whose stories include some of the legends surrounding these faith-filled people. A wealth of suggestions are given to integrate the material: questions, crafts, puzzles, games, plays, and prayer services are some of the options. The legacy of these people is still alive today in the religious orders they founded, the prayers and spiritual writings they left behind, but most of all in the way in which they lived the faith, often pioneering a life-style that was opposed to the ideals of their day. Our children need these holy models and heroes."

Margrit Anna Banta, Pastoral Minister
Holy Trinity Church, Norfolk, VA

"Sr. Kathleen's presentation of the lives of the saints is a most effective approach in capturing the interest of not only children but adults as well. The high points in a saint's life are simply presented, building up the biographical life sketch to keep the reader's attention. Also, this is written keeping the busy teacher in mind. Lesson plans have a variety of choices so that all the teacher has to do is choose from a list of excellent suggestions, even to the closing prayer. Hopefully, Sr. Kathleen will continue writing other books like this, for there are many more saints that have much to tell us."

Sr. Jane Reehorst, BVM

"Extraordinary courage, inspired conviction, and strong choices made for love are heroic qualities which have attracted people throughout generations. In the saints, that is, men and women whose lives were focused on God, these qualities are admirable and imitable. Sr. Kathleen Glavich, in her book, *Saints for Children*, has translated for all of us the deeds of saints into stories, plays, games, and songs that make these virtuous heroes once again present and real in our lives. This book is a fine resource for parents, teachers, homilists, and for children of all ages."

Suzanne Nelson
Director, Center for Pastoral Theology and Ministry
Notre Dame College of Ohio

SAINTS
FOR CHILDREN

- Stories
- Activities
- Prayer Services

KATHLEEN GLAVICH, SND

XXIII

TWENTY-THIRD PUBLICATIONS
Mystic, CT 06355

Second printing 1999

Twenty-Third Publications
185 Willow Street
P.O. Box 180
Mystic, CT 06355
(860) 536-2611
(800) 321-0411

ISBN 0-89622-738-3
Library of Congress Catalog Card Number 97-60848
Printed in the U.S.A.

Dedication

To Jane Samuelson,
my mentor and friend,
who is an example of a modern saint.

Contents

Dear Teacher or Parent,

Today, when youth are sadly in need of heroes, the church offers them a host of inspiring men and women: the saints. Many people have been motivated to lead a better life upon hearing the stories of the saints. St. Ignatius of Loyola was stirred to change his vain and empty life into one filled with zeal for the Lord when he read about the lives of Christ and the saints. We do our children a great service by introducing them to the outstanding members in their family of faith, the family of God.

These people in heaven show us that eternal life is within our grasp. Even more importantly, they demonstrate how to go about achieving it. Children can learn from the saints how to love God and others in this world. They can learn faith, hope, and charity. Most inspiring for some children are the stories of those saints who experienced a conversion, such as Augustine or Camillus de Lellis. It also is heartening for children (and us) to know that some saints battled a fault or character weakness all their lives, such as Francis de Sales, who had to curb his temper.

In God's plan of salvation the saints can intercede for us, and we pray to them for help. The church encourages devotion to the saints by naming saints patrons of countries and occupations. Mary, under the title of the Immaculate Conception, is the patroness of the United States. Her husband, St. Joseph, is the patron of workers. Saints are also invoked for certain diseases, ailments, and problems. St. Blase is the patron of diseases of the throat, while St. Jude has the distinction of helping with hopeless cases.

The universal church honors the saints in its liturgical year. We celebrate a cycle of the feast days of the saints in our Masses and in the prayer of Christians. The *Catechism of the Catholic Church* reminds us that in every Eucharist we are united with all the saints in the heavenly liturgy. For centuries Christians have given their children saints' names, thereby placing them under a particular saint's patronage. Places and geographical features are sometimes named for saints, for example, San Francisco for St. Francis of Assisi, St. Louis for St. Louis IX, and Mount Saint Helens for St. Helen. Buildings, such as St. Luke's Hospital, organizations, such as the St. Vincent de Paul Society, and parishes are also named for saints.

It is good to honor the saints, to name things after them, to set up shrines for them, and to wear their medals. But as the Dutch theologian Erasmus wrote, "No devotion to the saints is more acceptable and more proper than if you strive to live their virtue."

We are seeing a renewed interest in the saints today, along with a resurgence of interest in the spiritual life. This is logical, because as we search for God, as well as for the meaning of life, the saints show us the love of God in flesh and blood.

This book presents some of the greatest saints who have made an impact on the life of the church, one for each month of the year. Each story is followed by questions for discussion, suggested activities, a craft, a playlet about the saint, a prayer service, and pencil or crayon activities. Any of this material can be duplicated for an entire class.

On the next page is an introduction for children called "Saints: Our Friends and Models." You might want to read it to your class (or duplicate it for them) before you begin teaching them about the saints. Included in the introduction is a list of activities to help you and the children you teach learn more about these holy men and women. A list of helpful resources can be found at the back of the book.

Saints: Our Friends and Models

Maybe when you were younger you had an invisible friend. While this friend was only imaginary, you do have thousands of unseen but real friends who are ready to help you: the saints. These are members of the church—men, women, and children—who have gone before you into heaven. The saints are very much interested in you, because all people who are united in Christ are related in a special way. We are called the Communion of Saints. This includes people on earth, in purgatory, and in heaven.

Saint comes from the Latin word *sanctus*, which means holy. The saints have already won the race of life and are enjoying their reward of eternal life. Now they are rooting for you. They want you to love God and others so much that you can share the peace and joy which they have forever. The saints have the power to pray to God for you so that you might have the grace you need to live a good life.

You probably like to know about relatives and to hear family stories. The saints are your ancestors in the family of God, and it is good to know about them. They are as unique and real and wonderful as the people you know on earth. Just like the members of your family tree, the saints have different personalities, different talents, and different callings. They come from all countries and all centuries. Some will appeal to you more than others. You might make some your best friends—for instance, the saint you may have been named for, who is called your patron saint.

Like you, the saints and the way they practiced the faith are influenced by the customs and attitudes of their times. For this reason some things about their lives will seem strange to you. Basically, though, the saints had the same needs, dreams, difficulties, temptations, joys, sorrows, and experiences that you and all human beings have.

The stories of the saints have been told by Christians down through the ages. As the stories were repeated, some admirers added fantastic tales or exaggerated the facts. They wanted to stress what great people the saints were. Because of this, we sometimes have a hard time knowing what is historically true. We do know, though, that the saints lived remarkable lives or they wouldn't have been remembered.

Hearing about the saints and their love for God moves us to love God more too. The saints are heroes who inspire us to be better persons. They show us that it is possible to be holy, and they teach us the way. The saints are our models. By imitating them we become more like Christ.

The church has an official process, called canonization, by which a person is declared a saint. Besides the canonized saints, there are thousands upon thousands of other "saints" who are in heaven because of the good and holy lives they led while here on earth. This group likely includes your great-grandparents and other relatives. With the help of the saints, may you, too, arrive someday at your heavenly home and be called "saint"!

Activities on the Saints

Consider including the lives of the saints in your home or classes in the following ways:

1. Celebrate the feast days of the saints, especially the patron saints of your children. Display pictures of the saints. If possible, participate in the Eucharist. Be ingenious in creating rituals and symbols. For St. Peter's feast, you might make rock candy; for St. Patrick's Day, try adding green food coloring to milk.

2. Celebrate Halloween as the eve of the Feast of the Hallowed (the saints). Have a party where the children dress as saints. Let them give short reports, skits, or poems about the saints.

3. Read biographies of the saints or view videos of their lives as a class or family.

4. Display statues and pictures of the saints.

5. Point out statues, stained-glass windows, and art that depict saints in your parish church. Have the children find out about these saints.

6. Give holy cards of the saints. These may be purchased or homemade.

7. Pray to the saints. Use the prayer of the saint's feast day liturgy. At times, pray a litany of saints.

8. Say prayers of the saints.

9. Help the children draw pictures or make puppets or cutout dolls of the saints.

10. Work together to compile a list of places, geographical features, buildings, and institutions named for saints.

11. Have the children collect songs and poems about the saints.

12. Give the children an idea of how saints are canonized using the following information.

The Process of Canonization

Some people have been officially declared saints by the church. The process of adding a person to the canon, or list, of saints is called *canonization.* It involves proving that the person had heroic virtue or was a martyr.

At first, the early Christians honored the martyrs as saints. Then, in 993, bishops began canonizing saints and assigned each a feast-day, usually the day the saint died and was born into eternal life. Since 1234, only the pope has canonized saints.

For many years canonization was like a trial. Promoters of the saint faced a promoter of the faith, or devil's advocate, who made objections to the person's sanctity.

In 1983 the process changed. Today the local bishop gathers evidence and sends it to the Congregation for the Causes of Saints in Rome. If the cause is accepted, the congregation appoints a relator, someone who sees that an account of the candidate's life and virtues is written. The account is studied by historians, theologians, cardinals, and bishops. If approved, the cause goes to the pope for his decision. If the pope approves, the person is declared venerable. Then, if one miracle has been worked through his or her intercession, the pope beatifies the person, who is then called blessed. We are encouraged to pray to him or her. If the person passes more examinations and one more miracle is worked, the pope may officially declare that the person is recognized as a saint. (For martyrs no miracles are required.)

The canonization is usually held at a Mass in St. Peter's in Rome. A large picture of the saint is hung in St. Peter's Square for the occasion. Sometimes the pope canonizes a person when he is visiting his or her country.

St. Elizabeth Ann Seton
Mother of the American Church

August 28, 1774–January 4, 1821

In Emmitsburg, Maryland is a large rock where Elizabeth Ann Seton used to sit and teach children about God. She wore a black dress and a bonnet, the garb of Italian widows. This was the habit of the Sisters of Charity, the community she founded and the first American community of sisters.

Mother Seton's students would probably have been surprised to know that their teacher once wore elegant gowns and went to grand balls in New York. She was from a well-to-do, Episcopalian family. Her father, Dr. Bayley, was a respected physician. Her mother died when Elizabeth was three. The woman who became the stepmother of Elizabeth and her older sister Mary was not very loving. They were raised for the most part on their uncle's farm.

An Ill-fated Marriage

When Elizabeth was nineteen, she and William Seton were married. He was in the shipping business and was six years older than she. The two were very much in love. As members of New York's upper class, they once helped plan George Washington's birthday party. In their house on Wall Street, they were neighbors to Alexander Hamilton, the first secretary of the treasury. Elizabeth, however, had a heart for the poor. With her sister-in-law Rebecca, she formed a society of women who provided for needy widows and orphans. The two women did so much good that people called them the Protestant Sisters of Charity.

Elizabeth's blissful wedded life did not last long. After two children, and with another on the way, she inherited seven more. Will's father had died, leaving him responsible for his younger brothers and sisters. After her baby was born, Elizabeth moved into Will's father's house which was larger than theirs. She had two more children, took in needy relatives, and at one time found herself running a household of eighteen members. She worked very hard, teaching the younger children, nursing them through sicknesses, and being a business secretary for Will.

Then financial problems began. Pirates attacked the Seton ships, and goods were lost. The Setons became bankrupt. At the same time, Will's nagging cough became worse. He had tuberculosis, a lung disease that in those days usually led to an early death.

In hopes of improving Will's health, Elizabeth and he, with their oldest daughter, eight-year-old Anna, sailed to Italy. They planned to stay at the home of the Filicchis. The Filicchi brothers, Antonio and Filippo, were Will's business friends. The voyage was rough and took almost two months. Then came a blow. When the ship reached Italy, the Setons were not allowed to land because the yellow fever had been in New York. They had to stay in an old fort offshore for a month so they would not spread this disease.

The prison-like stone fort was cold and

damp. Anna jumped rope to keep warm. Will grew worse. Only about a week after the family was allowed to leave the fort, he died. At the age of twenty-nine, Elizabeth was left a widow with five children no older than eight.

Becoming a Catholic

Elizabeth and Anna stayed with the Filicchis. These good Catholic people shared their home, their money, and their faith. They explained their beliefs to Elizabeth. In the Filicchi house was a chapel, and Elizabeth was drawn to Jesus' presence in the Blessed Sacrament. She wrote to Rebecca Seton, "How happy we would be if we believed what these dear souls believe: that they possess God in the Sacrament and that he remains in their churches and is carried to them when they are sick!" Elizabeth, who had not really known a mother, was also attracted to the Catholic devotion to Mary as our heavenly mother.

After several months, Elizabeth and Anna sailed home under the protection of Antonio Filicchi. Back in New York, Elizabeth struggled with her desire to become a Catholic. At that time in New York, most Catholics were lower class. They were often dirty, poor, and ignorant. Elizabeth studied the faith, prayed, and even wrote the Archbishop John Carroll, the first bishop of the United States, for advice. In 1805 she became a Catholic at St. Peter's.

Most of Elizabeth's friends and family were shocked and dismayed. When she most needed help, they snubbed her. Her children were mocked at school. Elizabeth's sister-in-law Cecilia also became Catholic, which didn't help the situation. To support her family Elizabeth tired to teach and once made her home a boarding house for students. Sadly, both jobs failed because people did not wish to have their children in the care of a Catholic.

One day a young priest invited Elizabeth to open a school for girls in the Catholic town of Baltimore, Maryland. A year later Elizabeth and her family moved to Baltimore. Soon she had ten students at her boarding school. Other women joined her in prayer and teaching.

The First American Community of Sisters

Archbishop John Carroll knew of Elizabeth's desire to be a sister. At his suggestion she began a religious community. She made religious vows in 1809 and became known as Mother Seton. That same year she decided to open a school for poor children made possible by a donation from a rich young man. She, Anna, and her sisters moved to Emmitburg from Baltimore. They walked the fifty miles there beside a covered wagon.

At first the sisters stayed in a log cabin in the mountains. Then they moved into a stone house, which was crowded. Their life was hard. They had to haul firewood and wash their clothes in a creek. Finally, the White House was built. This was a convent and school on the sisters' property in St. Joseph's Valley. It was the beginning of the American parochial school system. Cecilia and Anna both joined the community. By 1818 the community had grown and there were fifty-seven boarders. In 1814, at Archbishop Carroll's request, Mother Seton sent four sisters to work in an orphanage in Philadelphia. They began the first American Catholic orphanage. After her death, Mother Seton's sisters also began the first Catholic hospital in America.

Mother Seton always remained a mother. She agreed to be a religious only if she could still carry out her duties as a mother. She also became a mother to the sisters in her community and to the children and others she taught.

Mother Seton's problems continued. A priest in charge of her community made bad decisions and even planned to have Mother Seton replaced as head of the community. Mother Seton also suffered when two of her daughters, Anna and Rebecca, and her three young sisters-in-law died of tuberculosis.

Eventually, in 1821, Mother Seton died of the same disease at the age of forty-six. She was canonized in 1975, the first native-born saint of the United States.

What Do You Think?

- How did people hurt Elizabeth? How did they help her?
- Why was Elizabeth Ann Seton canonized a saint?
- What good came out of Elizabeth's suffering?
- What do you think made Elizabeth become a Catholic?
- How can you share your faith with others?
- What are some things to do when making an important decision?

Things to Do

1. List the different roles Elizabeth Ann Seton had in her life.
2. Compose a prayer to help you follow the vocation to which God is calling you.
3. Write a report on another American Catholic saint, missionary, or pioneer, or on some other aspect of the church in America, such as the National Shrine.
4. Locate New York City, Baltimore, and Italy on a map or globe.
5. Write a composition about the value of Catholic schools.
6. With a classmate, hold an interview with Elizabeth, Will, or Anna about Elizabeth's life.
7. Consult books and sketch a scene or two from Elizabeth's life.
8. Sing or listen to a song about Mary or about the Blessed Sacrament.

Craft: Chalice and Host

From colored construction paper draw and cut out a host, a chalice, grapes, and two or three stalks of wheat. Arrange them on a sheet of white construction paper and then glue them down. You might prefer to draw the symbols on white paper and then color them with crayon, paint, or markers.

A Playlet: A Visit to Mother Seton

Characters: Elizabeth, her sister Mary

(Elizabeth and Mary are seated.)

Mary: I can't tell you how good it is to see you, Betsy. Four years is a long time.

Elizabeth: Yes. Now you can report to the rest of the family and my friends that I am doing well here in Emmitsburg. That is, those who don't hold a grudge against me for becoming a Catholic.

Mary (gesturing to room): This house is beautiful, so large and clean.

Elizabeth: We call it the White House. It's a relief after the cramped quarters of the stone house.

Mary: How many of you are here?

Elizabeth: There are eighteen sisters and almost thirty boarders. We have about twenty day students. My own children, though, always come first in my life. That was the agreement.

Mary: The children really love you. They almost knocked you over when they ran to you earlier.

Elizabeth: I love them too. I'm so glad I can teach them, not just reading and history, but about God and how to live well. Just yesterday I was telling the older girls a fable. A butterfly who was always getting its wings singed in candle flames went to the owl for advice. The owl said, "As soon as you see smoke, stay away!"

Mary (laughing): That's good advice. Too bad I don't always follow it. Who would ever have thought that my sister, the belle of New York balls, would found a Catholic community of sisters and start a Catholic school?

Elizabeth: I certainly never dreamed of it. God turned my life upside down when Will, Anna, and I went to Italy. The Filicchis who took us in changed my life. They still support me in many ways. My friend Julia is very generous with donations, too.

Mary: You look happy, Betsy, but a little pale. Are you well?

Elizabeth: Well, it seems that the family disease, tuberculosis, has caught up with me. And I don't think I'll ever get over losing Will and this year, Anna. She was so young. Just like dear Cecilia, Will's sister, who followed me here to Maryland.

Mary: Your little Rebecca seems to be in pain.

Elizabeth: Yes. She fell on the ice several months ago and never said anything. The doctors say her injured hip will just get worse.

Mary (shaking head): A mother has many heartaches.

Elizabeth: So does the Mother of a community. But I'm fortunate in having friends like Father Dubois and Father Bruté to see me through them. And I find such comfort in the Blessed Sacrament. In the end I can only marvel at God's plans.

Mary: I wish I had your faith.

Elizabeth: I wish you did, too. Come now. I want to show you the farmyard, our little cemetery, and my mountain and valley.

(The women rise and exit.)

Prayer Service

Song: "All I Ask of You," "Jesus Is Life," "We Walk by Faith," or "Proclaim the Good News"

Leader: St. Elizabeth's faith was so strong that she could cope with her trials. She had courage to do what she thought was right when others criticized and condemned her. She had energy to begin anew and to start new things. She was full of zeal because she was full of love for God. St. Peter encouraged the early Christians to have this kind of faith.

Reader: 1 Peter 1:1–9 (Our faith in Jesus and love of him leads to salvation and joy.)

Leader: People of faith brought St. Elizabeth to the Catholic Church, and she brought others. Let us pray that our faith may be a strong light that attracts other people to God.

All: Holy Spirit, thank you for the gift of faith.

Leader: Help me to make it grow by practicing it, by praying, and by living according to what Jesus taught.

All: Help me to learn more about my faith through religion classes, books, and other people.

Leader: Help me to share my faith with others by talking with them about what I believe.

All: May I always treasure my faith and be proud of it. Amen.

America's "First" Lady

St. Elizabeth Ann Seton was a pioneer in many ways. List the firsts of her and her community:

1. _____

2. _____

3. _____

4. _____

5. _____

The Story of Her Life

Think of a title for a biography of St. Elizabeth Ann Seton. Print it on the book below and design a cover. On the lines below, write a summary of the book that would be printed on the inside flap.

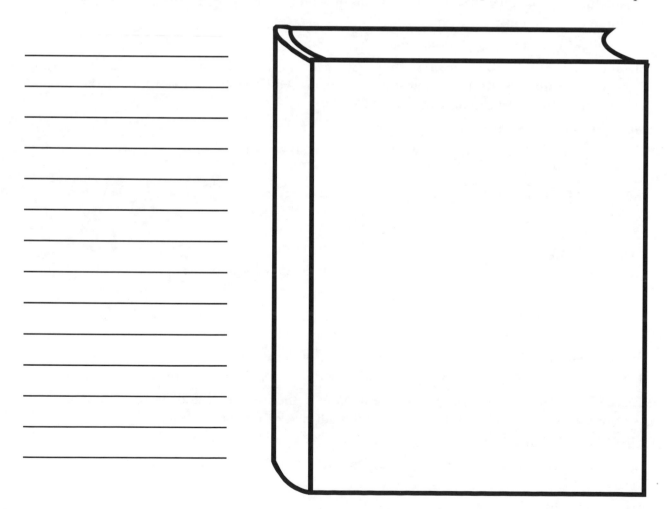

St. Peter: Prince of Apostles

First century

Who ever would have thought that a fisherman from a town in Galilee would be the first leader of the church? It was, however, God's plan to choose Simon from Capernaum to follow Jesus as an apostle and then to be the head of the church. Simon the fisherman is now St. Peter.

The "Rock" of the Church

According to John's gospel, it all began when Simon's brother Andrew claimed that he had found the Messiah. He brought Simon to meet Jesus, who gave Simon the name Peter, which means "rock." Later Jesus stated that he would found his church on this rock, which would be a strong foundation.

Luke's gospel tells us that when Jesus was talking to a crowd, he got into Simon's boat and asked him to take him a short distance from the shore. That way he could speak to the people more easily. When Jesus finished speaking, he told Simon to go out into the deep water and lower his nets. Simon explained that they had caught nothing all night, but he did as Jesus said. Simon's obedience paid off. So many fish were caught that the nets were tearing. Simon fell at Jesus' knees and said, "Depart from me, Lord, for I am a sinful man." And Jesus told him, "From now on you will catch people." Peter, Andrew, and their fishing partners, James and John, left everything to follow Jesus.

In the gospels of Matthew and Mark, the story is told this way: One day as Peter and Andrew were casting a net into the Sea of Galilee, Jesus walked by. He invited them, "Come after me, and I will make you fishers of people." Immediately the two brothers followed him and became his apostles.

As an apostle, Peter was with Jesus throughout his public life. He heard Jesus' teachings firsthand. He was an eyewitness to Jesus' miracles. In fact, Jesus once cured Peter's mother-in-law of a fever. Along with James and John, Peter was one of the three favored apostles who were with Jesus on special occasions: the raising of the daughter of Jairus, the transfiguration of Jesus, and the agony in the garden.

Peter showed signs of leadership. He sometimes spoke for the apostles. Once when Jesus asked them, "Who do you say I am?" it was Peter who replied, "You are the Messiah, the Son of the living God." In response to this act of faith, Jesus promised to give Peter the keys of the kingdom. In other words, Peter would have authority in the church on earth. For this reason pictures and statues of Peter often show him holding keys. These words of Jesus are also the source of the legend that St. Peter stands at the gates of heaven letting people in or refusing them entrance.

Peter made another noteworthy act of faith. After Jesus explained that those who ate his flesh and drank his blood would have eternal life, many followers left him. Jesus asked his apostles, "Do you also want to leave?" Peter promptly replied, "To whom shall we go? You have the words of eternal life. We believe that you are the Holy One of God."

Overcoming Fear and Weakness

Although Peter had strong faith and loyalty to Jesus, he was impulsive, that is, he acted without thinking. This got him into trouble. One night when the apostles were on a boat tossed about by a rough sea, Jesus came walking across the water. The men thought they were seeing a ghost and were terrified. Jesus reassured them, "Take courage. It is I." Peter challenged, "Lord, if it is you, command me to come to you on the water." When Jesus said, "Come," Peter stepped out of the boat onto the sea and began to walk on it. Suddenly he realized how strong the wind was. Peter became frightened and began to sink. He called out, "Lord, save me." Jesus caught him by the hand and scolded, "O you of little faith, why did you doubt?" Then they both got into the boat.

Peter was rebuked by Jesus another time. Jesus had been talking about having to go to Jerusalem to suffer and die. Peter, trying to prevent this terrible thing, tempted Jesus not to go through with his mission. Jesus replied, "Get behind me, Satan!"

On the night before Jesus died, Peter showed both great love and great weakness. At the Last Supper when Jesus was washing the feet of the apostles, Peter refused to let him wash his feet. Jesus told him that unless he let him wash his feet, he would have no share with him. Then Peter went to the other extreme and exclaimed, "Not only my feet, but my hands and head too!" Later that evening when Jesus and the apostles were eating, Peter boldly proclaimed that he would lay down his life for Jesus. Then Jesus made the sad prediction that before the rooster crowed, Peter would deny him three times.

After the supper, Jesus, Peter, James, and John went to a garden on the Mount of Olives. There Jesus prayed, dreading the ordeal he was about to undergo. Instead of offering him companionship, his friends fell asleep three times. John's gospel tells us that when the mob arrested Jesus, Peter cut off the ear of the high priest's servant. And as Jesus was taken away, Peter followed at a distance. In the courtyard people identified Peter as a follower of Jesus three times, and each time Peter denied knowing Jesus. The rooster crowed, and Peter cried, deeply regretting that he had fulfilled Jesus' prophecy.

But Jesus understood Peter's fear and weakness and still favored him. After Jesus rose from the dead, Peter was the first apostle to go into the empty tomb. The risen Lord appeared to him. Later, Jesus appeared to the apostles while they were fishing. In their presence he allowed Peter to make up for his threefold denial. Three times Jesus asked Peter, "Do you love me?" Three times Peter answered, "Yes, Lord, you know that I love you." And three times Jesus told Peter to feed his sheep. Peter was to be the good shepherd who cared for the flock of God's people. He was to be the chief apostle and teach and govern Christ's church, leading it to holiness. The popes of the past two thousand years are his successors.

His Mission Begins

Peter began his mission on Pentecost. After the Holy Spirit came to the church, Peter went out to the people gathered in Jerusalem and delivered the first sermon about Christ the Lord. About three thousand people were baptized that day.

Like Jesus, Peter healed many people. Even his shadow passing by was believed to bring about healing. The Acts of the Apostles tells the story of Dorcas, a good woman who died. Her friends brought Peter to the house where she was. Weeping women showed him clothes Dorcas had made. Peter prayed, and Dorcas came back to life.

Peter led the church. Through a vision and the guidance of the Holy Spirit, Peter made a basic decision about its membership. The church would be not just for Jewish people, but for all people. It is believed that Peter also wrote the two letters named for him in the New Testament. These letters encourage the early Christians to be faithful.

Like Jesus, Peter was persecuted for spreading the Good News. Once when he was in prison, an angel appeared. Peter's chains fell off, and the angel led him past the guards to freedom.

In the end, Peter did lay down his life for the Lord. According to tradition, in about the year 64, Peter was sentenced to be crucified in Rome. Because Peter declared that he was not worthy of the same death as Jesus, he was crucified upside down. It is believed that his tomb is in Rome under St. Peter's Basilica, where the pope holds many of the church's solemn celebrations. In this basilica is a chair thought to be the one from which Peter presided over the Eucharist. The feast of February 22, called the Chair of St. Peter, celebrates Peter's authority. St. Peter has another feast day on June 29, which he shares with St. Paul, another great apostle.

What Do You Think?

• How did Peter show love for Jesus?

• How did Jesus show love for Peter?

• How was Peter a normal human being?

• How do you think Peter felt when Jesus asked Peter to follow him? When he saw Jesus work miracles? When he realized he had denied Jesus? When Jesus appeared to him after the resurrection?

• What is your favorite story about St. Peter? Why?

• How can you show respect for the head of the church today?

• What virtues and qualities do the leaders of the church need?

• It is said that the pope and bishops save souls with the crook (staff) of the shepherd or the hook of the fisherman. How is this saying related to Peter?

Things to Do

1. Find out about your own pope and/or bishop. Write a brief report.

2. Read a few verses from the letters of Peter and write a summary of them.

3. On a clean, dry rock, letter a saying of faith in Christ with a marker. You might print "You are the Son of God," "Jesus is Lord," or "Lord, I believe." Add decorations. Glue felt to the base of the rock to make it a paperweight.

4. Write a report about St. Peter's Basilica. Sketch it or make a model of it.

5. Draw a scene from Peter's life.

6. Resolve to pray for the leaders of the church.

7. Read some stories in the Bible about Peter:

   • Peter's profession of faith (Mark 8:27–30)

   • the Transfiguration of Jesus (Matthew 17:1–9)

   • the Agony in the Garden (Mark 14:32–50)

   • the tax money in the fish (Matthew 17:24–27)

   • the cure of the paralyzed man (Acts of the Apostles 3:1–10)

   • Peter's escape from prison (Acts of the Apostles 12:1–11)

Craft: Fish

A fish is a Christian symbol because the word *fish* in Greek is made of the initials of the phrase "Jesus Christ, Son of God, Savior." Draw the outline of a fish with white glue on a piece of plastic wrap, wax paper, or aluminum foil. Press a strand of yarn around the outline and cover this yarn with a layer of glue. Glue a loop of yarn about one inch long to the top. Let the glue dry for a few hours. Gently peel the hardened fish from the paper. String another strand of yarn through the loop and tie the ends so the fish can be hung in a window or worn.

A Playlet: On the Mountain

Characters: Peter, Andrew, Thomas, James, and John

(The apostles are talking after the resurrection, but before Pentecost.)

Andrew (to Peter): Brother, are you really sure you saw Jesus alive?

Peter: Absolutely. This was no ghost. I should know. I'll never forget the love in his eyes. How could he still favor me after I denied him, not once but three times?

Andrew: I'm sure he understood. Besides, you asked him once if we should forgive as many as seven times.

James: That's right. He answered, "Seventy-seven times," meaning always. That's the way he forgives us.

Andrew: I'm thrilled to hear you saw him, Peter, but how can this be?

Peter: Why should we be surprised he's alive? We knew he was special. James and John, remember when he took us up a mountain?

James (to Andrew and Thomas): Yes, we never mentioned it, but we had a very strange experience that day.

John: Suddenly Jesus was all bright and shining, even his clothes. We couldn't look at him. Then Moses and the prophet Elijah were with him talking to him.

Thomas: How could they be? They've been dead for years.

Andrew: What were they talking about?

Peter: About the suffering and death Jesus would have to undergo in Jerusalem.

Thomas: We should have made sure he never went there then.

Peter: I was so flabbergasted I didn't know what to say.

Andrew: Now that's a miracle. I've never known you to be speechless!

Peter: Well, I did blurt out something. I asked Jesus if we could make three tents on the mountain for the three of them.

John: While Peter was speaking, a bright cloud came over us and we heard a voice say, "This is my beloved Son. Listen to him."

Thomas: I would have been scared to death.

James: We were. We fell to the ground. But then Jesus touched us, and when we looked up, he was alone and looking like his normal self.

Peter: I'm positive we'll be seeing Jesus again. Who knows what he'll be asking us to do next? Whatever it is, I'm ready.

Andrew, James, John (with enthusiasm): Me too!

Thomas: Oh, if it were only true that Jesus still lives!

Peter: He does. Believe me. I'd stake my life on it.

Prayer Service

Song: "Do You Really Love Me?" "The Church's One Foundation," "For All the Saints," "Lord, You Have Come," or "Trust in the Lord"

Leader: Peter and the other apostles were privileged to witness Jesus' words and actions. They knew the wonder of being in his presence. They knew his love. Before he ascended, Jesus sent them to spread the Good News.

Reader: Matthew 28:18–20 (Jesus commissions the disciples.)

Leader: We too are sent to bring about God's kingdom. Under the leadership of Peter's successor, the Holy Father, we live by the teachings of Jesus and try to make him known and loved. Let us pray to the Holy Spirit for our church leaders that they may have the qualities they need to be good leaders.

All: Come, Holy Spirit, give them wisdom.

Come, Holy Spirit, give them courage.

Come, Holy Spirit, give them faith.

Come, Holy Spirit, give them hope.

Come, Holy Spirit, give them patience.

Come, Holy Spirit, give them dedication.

Come, Holy Spirit, give them a great love of Jesus.

Come, Holy Spirit, give them enthusiasm.

Leader: Now let us pray that we may have the same qualities.

All: Come, Holy Spirit, give us wisdom.

Come, Holy Spirit, give us courage.

Come, Holy Spirit, give us faith.

Come, Holy Spirit, give us hope.

Come, Holy Spirit, give us patience.

Come, Holy Spirit, give us dedication.

Come, Holy Spirit, give us a great love of Jesus.

Come, Holy Spirit, give us enthusiasm.

Fishing for Words

Find and circle twenty words related to St. Peter. They run across, down, and diagonally.

```
S O A P O S T L E M U N D P C
H J E S U S F A I T H L M O D
E M C R U C I F I X I O N P R
P L A Q V E S U P A D M N E I
H O P M O T H E R I N L A W H
E K E Y S T E N I X E D W C L
R O R A M I R O S T E L R O W
D E N I A L M I O I U U O E G
R E A L C R A O N U H E C E W
E G U E P K N I N C K O K V U
B R M I R A C L E S D E C K E
V O L E D O P E N T E C O S T
R E S L E T T E R S C I D U E
```

List of words to find:

POPE	**CHURCH**
FISHERMAN	**FAITH**
MOTHER-IN-LAW	**ROCK**
ROME	**ANDREW**
PENTECOST	**KEYS**
CAPERNAUM	**MIRACLES**
APOSTLE	**PRISON**
SIMON	**CRUCIFIXION**
DENIAL	**LETTERS**
SHEPHERD	**JESUS**

Words to Live By

Bishops today choose mottoes for themselves. Think of a motto that fits St. Peter. Write it in the box below and decorate it.

St. Joseph: Foster Father of Jesus

First Century

When God the Father planned to send his only Son to become a man, he needed someone to be a good foster father to Jesus and a good husband to Mary. He needed a man who was strong and gentle, dependable and loving, religious and practical, courageous and faithful. God made a wise choice. He chose Joseph of Nazareth to be the head of the Holy Family.

An Unexpected Birth

Joseph was a carpenter who at that time also did the work of a construction worker. He lived in the small town of Nazareth although he came from the royal line of King David. Since most Jewish men married before they were twenty, Joseph was probably in his late teens when he became betrothed to Mary, who also lived in Nazareth. This was a much more serious commitment than engagement is today. Suddenly Joseph's happy, uneventful life turned upside down. Before he and Mary came to live together, she was pregnant and Joseph knew he was not the father.

Poor Joseph. Apparently Mary, his bride-to-be, loved someone else. For some reason God kept Joseph in the dark during this time and let him experience shock, bewilderment, and pain. Being a good man, Joseph decided he could not wed Mary. Although according to the law she could be put to death, Joseph intended to break their engagement quietly.

After making this sad decision, Joseph fell asleep. An angel spoke to him in a dream and said, "Joseph, son of David, do not be afraid to take Mary as your wife. For it is through the Holy Spirit that this child has been conceived in her. She will bear a son and you are to name him Jesus, because he will save his people from their sins." The name Jesus means "God saves." With this news, Joseph took Mary into his home, but the young couple didn't live happily ever after there.

The emperor called for a census. Everyone was to go to the town of their ancestors to be registered. Joseph, a good citizen, had to journey south to Bethlehem, the city of David. Although it was almost time for Mary to have her baby, she went with him. When the two travelers arrived in Bethlehem, the inns were filled. Mary was about to have her baby at any time. Joseph must have dreaded the thought of her spending the night outside or with a crowd of strangers. Luckily, someone finally offered them a private place where animals were kept. There, Jesus, God's Son, known on earth as the son of Joseph the carpenter, was born. Mary laid him in a manger, a feedbox for animals. Joseph probably felt terrible that the son of God, under his protection, was born in such poor surroundings.

How Joseph must have wondered at this birth and how puzzled he must have been! His wonder increased when shepherds came to honor the child. They told a fantastic story of an angel who announced the news of the savior and sent them to find the child in the manger. They said they saw a host of angels singing "Glory to God in the highest!" Joseph was amazed at the shepherds' words. He was amazed again when wise men from the East visited and brought precious gifts for Jesus.

According to Jewish law, parents had to present their firstborn son to God at the Temple and offer a sacrifice. Obedient to religious laws, Joseph took Mary and Jesus to the Temple in Jerusalem to offer two young pigeons, the sacrifice of the poor. That day an old man named Simeon was sent to the Temple by the Spirit. God had promised him that he wouldn't die until he had seen the Messiah. On seeing Jesus, Simeon took him in his arms and praised God. He called the baby a light for the gentiles and the glory of the people Israel. Joseph and Mary were astounded at this stranger's words. Then Simeon blessed Mary and Joseph and foretold that the child would face opposition. He also foretold that because of this Mary would suffer as though a sword were piercing her heart. At hearing these predictions for the two people he loved most, Joseph must have been filled with sorrow.

Facing Hardships

The opposition began immediately. An angel appeared to Joseph in a dream and warned him that King Herod wanted to kill Jesus. He told Joseph to flee to Egypt and stay there until furthur notice. At once Joseph got up and took Mary and Jesus to Egypt. Fear for his son's life gave him courage to face the unknown. But now Joseph had to start a new life in a strange land. As the guardian of the family, he had to find a place to stay among strangers who spoke a different language. He had to find a job where he had no reputation.

The family stayed in Egypt until King Herod died and an angel revealed to Joseph in a dream that it was safe to return. Joseph intended to go to Judea where Bethlehem was. When he learned that Herod's son ruled there, however, he wisely took his family back to Nazareth in Galilee instead. There Joseph and Mary raised Jesus.

The Bible records one last crisis that Joseph had to face as the earthly father of Jesus. When Jesus was twelve he went with Joseph and Mary to celebrate the Passover in Jerusalem. On the way home Joseph and Mary looked for Jesus among the others in the caravan at the end of the first day. Realizing that Jesus was missing, Mary and Joseph returned to Jerusalem. There they looked for him for three long days. Finally, they found Jesus in the Temple speaking to the teachers there. He was amazing them with his knowledge. Mary asked him, "Son, why have you done this to us? Your father and I have been looking for you with great anxiety." Jesus replied, "Did you not know that I must be in my Father's house?" He was referring to his heavenly Father. This answer puzzled Mary and Joseph. Jesus went back with them to Nazareth and was obedient to them.

This story is the last time Joseph appears in the gospels. When Jesus died, he left Mary in the care of St. John, so Joseph must have died by then. If so, Joseph probably had a peaceful death with Mary and Jesus at his side. For this reason, St. Joseph is patron of happy deaths.

A Quiet Hero

Joseph lived a quiet life in Nazareth. None of his words are quoted in the Bible. Joseph, however, was certainly favored by God. What joy he must have had living with Mary and Jesus! It was Joseph who provided Jesus and Mary with food, clothing, and shelter. He taught Jesus the Jewish laws and customs and how to pray. He handed on to him the trade of a carpenter. Under Joseph's care and protection, Mary and Jesus lived safely and happily. Best of all, Joseph surrounded them with his love.

Because Joseph is the foster father of Jesus, he was made the patron of the universal church. He now watches over all of us who are the body of Christ. St. Joseph is also the patron of workers, and can teach us the value of work. He was an honest workman who served customers well and charged fair prices. He gave dignity to earning a living by the sweat of your brow and having callused hands. St. Joseph has a special feast day on May 1 called the Feast of St. Joseph the Worker.

St. Joseph is also known as the patron of fathers, treasurers, artisans, manual laborers, the poor, those in authority, priests and religious, travelers, prayer, and devotion to Mary. Mexico, Canada, Bohemia, Peru, and Belgium claim him as their patron saint. St. Joseph is also the patron of house hunters. People pray to him when they want to sell or buy a house. Some even bury a statue of him in the front lawn, or turn it to face the wall until their prayers are answered.

In art St. Joseph is often shown with a lily, which stands for purity. Sometimes he holds a flowering staff. This comes from a legend that the High Priest ordered all men who wished to wed Mary to put their staffs on the altar. The man whose staff blossomed would be her husband. It was Joseph's staff that bloomed. The flowers also stand for the fact that Joseph is the flower, or descendant, of the root of Jesse prophesied in Scripture. Jesse was King David's father.

The month of March is dedicated to St. Joseph, and so is Wednesday. The Bible calls Joseph righteous. His holiness makes him the greatest and most powerful saint after Mary.

What Do You Think?

• How did Joseph practice great faith? Why didn't God make things easier for him?

• What are some things Jesus might have learned from Joseph?

• What must Jesus' attitude have been toward his foster father?

• What characteristics of a good father did Joseph have?

• What do you think a day in the holy family's home at Nazareth was like?

• What people in particular could have a devotion to St. Joseph?

• When would it be good to pray to St. Joseph?

• Why is work good? How can you make your work valuable?

• Why is St. Joseph a powerful saint?

Things to Do

1. For St. Joseph's feast some people carry on an Italian custom of creating St. Joseph's table. They fill a table with food and distribute it to the needy. Do something for the poor on this day.

2. Write three things about your life that you don't understand. Pray for the grace to trust God in these matters.

3. Reflect on a time when you were asked to do something or endure something you didn't understand. Did any good come out of it?

4. Do something special for your father or someone who takes the place of your father.

5. Write a poem in honor of St. Joseph or a prayer to him for the church.

6. Make something religious out of wood, such as a cross or a plaque.

7. Act out an event from St. Joseph's life with family members or friends.

8. Find news items about people who act honestly and justly.

9. Repair something around the house.

10. Make a habit of praying "Jesus, Mary, Joseph."

11. Resolve to imitate St. Joseph's obedience.

Craft

On a piece of sandpaper draw a picture, symbols, or words related to St. Joseph or Jesus lightly with pencil. Color it heavily with crayons.

A Playlet: The Honest Craftsman

Characters: Joseph, Aaron, Seth

(Aaron and Seth are walking towards a shop where Joseph is working.)

Aaron: I tell you, you won't be disappointed with Joseph's work. He takes pride in his work and uses the best materials. Never cheats. You saw the yoke he made for my oxen.

Seth: Yes, what fine workmanship, but I bet his prices match.

Aaron: Don't worry. Joseph doesn't overcharge. And if you can't pay right away, he always works something out. Do you know Jacob?

Seth: The poor fellow with ten mouths to feed?

Aaron: Yes. When Jacob's house needed repair, Joseph worked on it for free. We're lucky to have such a man in town.

Seth: I heard Joseph has a son.

Aaron: Right. His name is Jesus, and he's following in his father's footsteps in more ways than one. A finer lad can't be found. One day he'll probably be taking over Joseph's business. Ah, Joseph! Shalom!

Joseph: Well, Aaron! Shalom! How's the yoke working out?

Aaron: Just fine. I brought you more business. This is Seth. He just moved here from Judea, though I don't know why anyone would move to Nazareth.

Joseph: Glad to meet you. I wish my wife Mary and my son Jesus were here. I gave the boy the day off to go with his mother to visit some sick friends. What can I do for you?

Seth: I'll be making a whole list. Right now, I just wanted to get acquainted. I saw you and Jesus at the synagogue last Sabbath, but I didn't know you were the best carpenters in Nazareth then!

Joseph: You must return tomorrow when Mary is here. Can you and your family join us for dinner? Mary loves to cook for guests, and her meals are delicious.

Seth: I would like that very much. I'm sure my wife Rachel and two sons would appreciate meeting our neighbors.

Joseph: Aaron, you're welcome to come too.

Aaron: Thank you. I always enjoy talking to Jesus. Such a mature young man—a chip off the old block, if you don't mind my saying so. **(Laughs)**

Joseph: Aaron has a rare sense of humor. You'll get used to it, Seth.

Aaron: Well, we'll see you tomorrow.

Seth: Good-bye.

Joseph: God be with you!

Prayer Service

Song: "Look Down to Us, St. Joseph," "St. Joseph Was a Just Man," or "St. Joseph, Great Protector"

Leader: St. Joseph is a model for trusting in God. Over and over he was asked to do things that he didn't understand. He acted in faith and played his part in the salvation of the world.

Reader: James 1:2–4 (Keep faith during trials.)

Leader: Let us ask St. Joseph, patron of the church, to pray that we, the members of Jesus' church, may have courage in difficulties and faith to go on. Let us pray from the Litany of St. Joseph for this intention. The response to each title of St. Joseph is "Pray for us."

> Saint Joseph,
>
> Illustrious son of David,
>
> Splendor of patriarchs,
>
> Spouse of the Mother of God,
>
> Chaste guardian of the Virgin,
>
> Foster father of the Son of God,
>
> Watchful defender of Christ,
>
> Head of the Holy Family,
>
> Joseph most just,
>
> Joseph most chaste,
>
> Joseph most prudent,
>
> Joseph most courageous,
>
> Joseph most obedient,
>
> Joseph most faithful,
>
> Mirror of patience,
>
> Lover of poverty,
>
> Model of all who work,
>
> Patron of the dying,
>
> Protector of holy church,
>
> Amen.

Leader: St. Joseph, you watched over the Holy Family with love and care. Please protect the church. Pray for its leaders, our Holy Father and bishops. Pray for all its members that we may make right decisions and help others live the right way.

All: Someday may I, my friends, and relatives all be joined with you in heaven as one, big, happy family. Amen.

St. Joseph's Flowers

Draw a lily or a flowering staff below.

A Quiet Hero

Work the crossword puzzle.

ACROSS

3. Joseph's trade
5. The universal institution that Joseph is patron of
7. King whose family Joseph came from
8. What Joseph was to name God's son
11. Man who taught and guarded Jesus
14. Flower associated with Joseph
15. Frequent messenger to St. Joseph
16. Where Joseph and Mary found Jesus when he was lost
17. Kind of father Joseph was to Jesus

DOWN

1. Joseph's wife
2. Joseph's month
4. Where Joseph lived
6. City of Joseph's ancestors
9. Group of people that Joseph is patron of
10. Old man who prophesied sorrows for Jesus and Mary
12. Kind of death we pray to St. Joseph for
13. Land Joseph fled to with Jesus and Mary

St. Catherine of Siena: Messenger for Christ

March 25, 1347–April 29, 1380

From the very start St. Catherine did not lead an ordinary life. For one thing she had twenty-three brothers and sisters, not counting her twin who died at birth. Her mother, called Lapa, was the daughter of a poet. Catherine's father was a wool-dyer. The house where the whole family lived in Siena, Italy still stands.

The Bride of Christ

When Catherine was six, she and her brother Stephen were walking home after visiting one of their married sisters. Above St. Dominic's church, Catherine saw Christ on a throne giving a blessing. With him were the apostles Peter, Paul, and John. Catherine stopped and stared. Her brother shook her, and the vision disappeared. Catherine began to cry.

After this vision, Catherine became very religious. Once she even packed some food and ran off to try living alone in silence and prayer as a holy hermit. At the end of the day, though, she returned home.

God meant so much to Catherine that she decided not to get married but to live as Christ's bride. This caused some trouble in the family. Her mother and older sister wanted Catherine to be like other young girls by showing interest in boys and in dressing up. Finally, Catherine settled the matter. She took the advice of a priest and cut off her beautiful hair!

Now Lapa was really upset. She could not understand her strange daughter. To make Catherine come to her senses, Lapa took her private room away and had her share Stephen's room. That way Catherine wouldn't be able to pray so much. Lapa also dismissed the servant, and Catherine had to cook for the large family. Catherine took these changes in stride. She prayed when Stephen was asleep or at work. And as she waited on her family, she pretended she was serving Jesus, Mary, and the apostles.

One day Catherine asked her parents if she could join the Mantellata, women who belonged to the Third Order of St. Dominic. They cared for the sick and the poor and lived in their own homes. They were older women, mostly widows, and wore the Dominican white robe and veil and black mantle. That's why they were called Mantellata.

Catherine's father, who had once seen a dove hovering over his daughter as she prayed in her room, gave his consent. Catherine made vows as a Mantellata when she was sixteen. From then on she lived in a narrow, private room above the kitchen in her family home. She spent her days in silence and prayer, leaving the house only for Mass. She hardly slept or ate and did such penance that Lapa worried about her.

Catherine's lifestyle must have pleased God though. God granted Catherine special favors in prayer. Jesus and the saints often appeared and talked with her. Jesus called her "My daughter, Catherine." Sometimes she went into ecstasy while she was with the Lord. That means her body would become stiff and she would not be able to see, hear, or feel.

One day Jesus appeared to Catherine and showed her that she really was like a bride to him. In the presence of his Blessed Mother, Mary, and the saints John and Paul, he held a mystical marriage. On Catherine's finger Jesus placed a ring that had a diamond encircled by four pearls. For the rest of her life Catherine could see it whenever she thought of him, which was most of the time.

Catherine's Public Ministry

For three years Catherine lived in prayer and silence by herself. Then one day Jesus told her that it was time for her to go out and love him in others. He wanted her to be the mother of all his children. And so Catherine started her public ministry. She began serving her family again and took food and supplies to the poor and sick. She worked in hospitals, nursing patients no one else wanted to care for. While working in a hospital for lepers, Catherine developed leprosy on her hands. There was a woman named Tecca in the hospital who ordered Catherine around and insulted her. Catherine always treated Tecca with loving kindness. At this woman's death, Catherine's leprosy disappeared.

Because Catherine was so close to God, the devil tried hard to tempt her. One day after fighting temptations, she asked Jesus, "Where were you when I was attacked by temptations?" Jesus answered, "I was right there in your heart." Jesus never left Catherine and showed much love for her. In one of her spiritual trances he even replaced her heart with his own.

Catherine attracted many followers. Men and women formed a group around her and accompanied her in her travels. She guided them in the spiritual life, helping them to see and correct their faults and to love God and one another. They were like her family and referred to her as Mama.

Blessed Raymond of Capua, a Dominican priest, was Catherine's spiritual director. He became her good friend and wrote her biography. Raymond and others wrote letters for Catherine. About four hundred of these letters still exist. Catherine also dictated a book called *Dialogue* in which she explains her way of living a spiritual life.

Reforming the Church

God used Catherine to help the church in a dark time of its history. She became involved in world politics and religious activities. Catherine became a prophet. She pointed out to people their errors and called them to repent. The sinners she converted filled the confessionals. Catherine was not afraid to remind people in high places, such as cardinals and rulers, that they were to be holy. Her mission of reforming the church even affected the pope.

For almost seventy years the popes had lived in Avignon, Paris. French kings had power over them. Back in Rome, some Italian dukes were taking the church's property. Catherine wrote Pope Gregory XI strong letters to convince him to return to Rome. She scolded him and even visited him in France. Some church officials did not believe that this mere woman was as wise or holy as people said. They questioned her and went away amazed at her knowledge.

Catherine reminded Pope Gregory that before he was elected he had made a secret vow to return to Rome. Because of her, the pope returned to Rome. When the next pope, Urban VI, was elected, Catherine became his advisor, too. Catherine was also a peacemaker. When Florence, a city in Italy, was feuding with the pope, she acted as a go-between.

Although slight and sickly, Catherine had much energy and courage. Once a mob in Florence, who called her the witch of Siena, came to her in a garden to kill her. The leader, who was carrying a sword, asked, "Where is this Catherine?" She answered, "Kill me, but I command you in the name of God that you do not harm any who are with me." Then she knelt and prayed. The mob left.

When some French bishops did not think that Pope Urban VI's election was valid, they elected their own pope. The church was split. Catherine, who loved the church, was distressed. She went to Rome and begged cardinals and kings to accept Urban VI as the true pope. She offered herself to God as a sacrifice for peace and unity in the church.

Catherine became very sick for three months. Then on April 29 with her friends around her, she died. She was only thirty-three years old. In 1975, this woman who had never gone to school was declared a doctor of the church. This is a title for someone who was outstanding in teaching and guiding the church. So far, St. Catherine and St. Teresa of Avila are the only women who bear this title. St. Catherine and St. Francis of Assisi are the patron saints of Italy.

What Do You Think?

- What about St. Catherine can we imitate?
- In what ways was Catherine favored by God?
- What was difficult about Catherine's life?
- Why did people follow Catherine?
- How can you show love for God as Catherine did?
- How can you help the church?

Things to Do

1. Write a report about the pope today.
2. Think of a way to serve your family with loving care.
3. Write a letter to someone who is sick or who would enjoy hearing from you.
4. Make a list of ways you can be a good influence on your friends.
5. Write down a conversation you might have with Jesus.
6. Draw a picture of a place where it would be easy for you to pray. When you pray, set it before you and think of yourself being there.
7. Resolve to pray for the pope and his special concerns.

Craft: Papal Flag

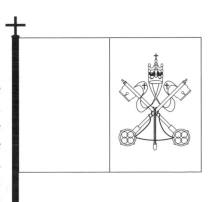

The papal flag has two equal vertical panels, one yellow and one white. In the white section there is a tiara (the pope's crown) and two keys. Fold a sheet of white paper in fourths and cut out one of the fourths. Turn the paper so that the missing fourth is on the bottom right. Draw a vertical line down the middle of the fourth above the missing piece. Color the left half yellow and draw and color the papal flag in the remaining half. To make the staff roll the blank half of the paper up to the flag and tape it together. On the leftover piece of paper, draw a cross and cut it out. Tape or staple it to the top of the flag.

A Playlet: A Saint Meets the Pope

Characters: St. Catherine, Pope Gregory XI

(Catherine and the pope are walking through a garden.)

Catherine: Holy Father, the city of Florence and the other cities in Italy do not really want to fight you. They sent me here to be a peacemaker. The demands you impose on them for peace, however, are impossible. I have failed in my mission.

Pope: The Florentine ambassadors say that they have nothing to do with you. Is this the truth?

Catherine: No, Holy Father. I offered to be a mediator, and Florence accepted my offer. I can't explain the ambassadors' attitude. In any case, this gives us a chance to discuss another matter.

Pope: I can guess what it is. Your letters are a mountain on my desk. Never has anyone pestered me quite so much or so persuasively. My daughter, I don't see what difference it makes whether I live here in Avignon or in Rome. The popes have been here now for almost seventy years.

Catherine: Without your presence in Italy, the papal states are being stolen away little by little. And because you are in France, people fear that you are under the control of the French government. The pope should be free to be father of all people everywhere.

Pope: I can function in France just as well as in Italy.

Catherine: But, Holy Father, it's time to fulfill what you have promised. Remember your vow.

Pope (shocked): How do you know about my vow to return to Rome? I never told anyone. Never mind. I've heard about you, Catherine, and the strange and wonderful things you do in Siena. My theologians, who at first were suspicious of you, were dumbfounded by your knowledge when they interviewed you. I believe that you were sent by God and speak for God.

Catherine: Then you will return to Rome?

Pope: As soon as I can get things in order, I will set sail.

Catherine: God be praised! The church will be so grateful, Holy Father.

Pope: And they will be grateful to you. Pray for me, Catherine.

Prayer Service

Song: "Only This I Want," "The Center of My Life," "Only in God," or "My God and My All"

Leader: St. Catherine loved Jesus with her whole heart. She enjoyed being alone with him in prayer. She was grateful for receiving him in Holy Communion. Jesus taught Catherine that she was to love him in words and in deeds. She was to love him in others. This is the message found in the story of Jesus' visit to the house of Martha and Mary in the village of Bethany.

Reader: Luke 10:38–42 (We are to show God's love in the two ways Martha and Mary did.)

Leader: St. Catherine knew how to live Martha and Mary's way. She was busy serving the church, but her heart was always fastened on Jesus. Let us pray to be like her.

All: St. Catherine, who guided so many people to holiness, pray for us.

Leader: Ask for us the grace to love God with all our heart and to love God in our neighbor.

All: Help us to be kind, thoughtful, and helpful.

Leader: Give us the interest and enthusiasm to work for the church in our family, school, and parish.

All: May we have the courage to live for Christ in the way Christ taught. Amen.

St. Catherine Acrostic

Use the clues to fill in the acrostic.

1. Saint whose order Catherine joined

2. What Catherine liked to do most

3. Country Catherine is patron of

4. Where Jesus was during her temptations

5. What she dictated in order to guide people

6. Her spiritual director and follower

7. What Christ considered her to be to him

8. Town Catherine was from

9. Catherine persuaded him to move to Rome

__ __ __ __ __ __ __   **C**

      __ __   **A** __

      __   **T** __ __ __

      H __ __ __

__ __ __ __   **E** __ __

      R __ __ __ __ __

      __ __   **I** __ __

      __ __ __   **N** __

      __ __ __   **E**

Two Loves

In the first heart write a prayer telling God of your love. In the second heart draw a way you can show love for God by helping someone.

St. Isidore: Holy Farmer

1070–May 15, 1130

Farmers sometimes hold a procession on Isidore's feast day, May 15, carrying a statue of St. Isidore into their fields. They also do this at times when their crops are threatened by drought, insects, or disease. Farmers look to Isidore for help because he understands their needs. He, too, was a farmer who depended on the weather and good crops for his living.

A Life of Labor

Isidore belonged to a poor family and had little education. He was a farm laborer from the time he was a boy and sent to work for a landowner named John de Vergas. He worked for this same man all of his life. The property of Señor de Vergas was just outside the city of Madrid in Spain.

Every morning Isidore went to Mass and then walked to work. He toiled on the land, plowing it, sowing seed, and harvesting the crops. He cared for the livestock. No matter what he was doing, Isidore prayed. As he followed the plow, he spoke to God, his guardian angel, and the saints. On his free days he visited churches in the region.

Isidore was a good worker, and his crops flourished. There is a story that other workers became jealous. They complained to Señor de Vergas that Isidore came to work late. This was true because sometimes Isidore stayed at church after Mass praying. His boss wanted to check for himself. One morning he hid behind some bushes and watched. Isidore was late, but Señor de Vergas saw that as he began

plowing, two angels with white oxen plowed with him. No wonder Isidore always got his work finished and finished well!

Isidore married Maria Torribia, a woman who was as holy as he was. She, too, is honored as a saint. The couple had one child, a son. According to a story, the boy fell into a well one day and died, but Isidore brought him back to life. This son did die young, and Isidore and Maria felt the pain of his loss as any parents would.

Isidore's Concern for the Poor

Isidore and Maria, though not well-off themselves, were good to the poor. They shared the food they had from the land Isidore worked. When Isidore saw beggars at the gate, he gave them his food and then ate what was left. It is said that Isidore once was invited to a dinner given by a wealthy man for a church organization. All the members left for the man's house right after church, except Isidore, who lingered in prayer. As Isidore finally began walking to the house, some beggars joined him. When they reached the house, they found that the meal had already been served. A portion had been set aside for Isidore, and he shared this with his hungry companions. Somehow there was enough for all!

According to another legend, Isidore had a similar concern for animals. One wintry day Isidore was carrying a sack of corn grain to the mill to be ground into flour. He passed a flock of birds huddled together. They were starving because the frozen ground kept them from finding food. Kindhearted Isidore opened his sack and spread half his grain on the ground for the birds. The men who were with him made fun of him for doing this. Isidore, however, had the last laugh. When they got to the mill, his sack was still full, and when the grain was ground, Isidore had twice as much flour as he should have had from one sack.

Rewarded in Death

Isidore lived the ordinary life of a poor person. He worked hard and was a good man. God showed how pleasing Isidore's life was when he died. Isidore's body did not turn to dust. People all over then recognized that Isidore was a saint. They placed his mummified body along with Maria's in the church of St. Andrew in Madrid.

After his death, Isidore continued to help people. There's a story that in 1211 he helped the King of Castile in Spain win a war. Isidore appeared to the king and revealed a secret path that enabled him to surprise and defeat the enemy. Four hundred years later, King Philip III of Spain became seriously ill. The doctors had no hope. The people brought Isidore's body in procession to the king. By the time it entered the sickroom, the king had recovered. He gave Isidore credit for his healing and urged that he be canonized. In 1612 Isidore was declared a saint along with Ignatius, Francis Xavier, Teresa of Avila, and Philip Neri. In Spain this group is known as "the five saints."

Isidore did more than plant seeds in the earth. All his life he sowed good works that made him a saint. His example encourages us to use whatever gifts we are given and to do well whatever we are called to do in life.

Isidore is the patron of Madrid as well as the patron of farmers and of the National Catholic Rural Life Conference of the United States. Through his intercession God blesses farmers' crops. Some of the food on your table might be the result of St. Isidore's prayers.

What Do You Think?

- Why did people regard Isidore as a saint?
- What do you think Isidore said to God, his guardian angel, and the saints?
- Isidore must have had great respect for the earth that yields our food. How can you show respect for the earth?
- Who are some workers whose jobs may seem lowly but are very important?
- How can you share what you have with others?
- How can family members help one another to be holy?
- What would St. Isidore say to us today?

Things to Do

1. Plant some seeds and watch the miracle of their growth. Don't forget to water them.
2. If you live near a farm, help a farmer by doing a chore for him or her. If not, say a prayer for farmers everywhere.
3. Learn more about farmers and their problems and joys by talking to one or by doing research.
4. Draw a picture about something in St. Isidore's life.
5. Write down a conversation St. Isidore and St. Maria might have had one day.
6. Spend an extra five minutes in prayer today.
7. Resolve to do your best in the tasks you undertake this week.

Craft: Cornucopia

Make a miniature cornucopia (horn of plenty) to remind you of St. Isidore. Take a four- or five-inch square of brown paper and roll it into a cone. Use a staple or tape to secure the cone. Form fruit and vegetables (including your favorites) out of colored clay, or make some out of papier mâché and paint when dry. Insert the produce in the horn.

A Playlet: On the Way to the Mill

Characters: Narrator, Isidore, Juan, Pedro

(The four men are walking down the road carrying sacks of corn on their shoulders.)

Juan: I can't remember when it has ever been so cold. Look at those birds pecking at the frozen ground. They will starve to death if they don't freeze to death first.

Pedro: My nose and ears are frozen. Good thing we're almost to the mill.

Juan: There's Isidore lagging behind. He's always late. Late for work, late for meals. What's he doing now?

Pedro: He's spreading his corn on the ground for the birds. Look at them flocking around.

Juan: He's thrown away half his sack. Hey, Isidore! Maria won't like that. How's she going to make your meals the rest of this winter?

Isidore: Maria would do the same thing I'm doing.

Pedro: I'd say you've been in the sun too long, if there was a sun.

Juan: What a fool. Those birds can't pay you back or even thank you.

Isidore: But they are God's creatures. We are to care for them.

Pedro: Well, I'd rather care for myself first. It's not as though we're rich.

(Juan and Pedro walk on.)

Juan: I heard that Isidore feeds beggars at his house. Then he eats what is left. Isidore, friend of birds and beggars. The man is crazy.

Pedro: What I don't understand is how he can outwork us.

Juan: I know what you mean. He stays at church praying when he should be in the fields, yet his work is finished on time and his harvests are better than ours.

Pedro: Maybe we should start feeding beggars and birds.

Juan: Sure, Pedro, sure.

Narrator: When the men reached the miller, Isidore handed him a sack full of grain. After the corn was ground, Isidore left with twice the normal amount of flour. All Pedro and Juan could do was scratch their heads and wonder.

Prayer Service

Song: "We Plow the Fields and Scatter," "All Good Gifts," "America," "For the Beauty of the Earth," "Stewards of Earth," "Father, We Thank Thee," or "For the Fruits of His Creation"

Leader: St. Isidore knew the dignity of manual labor. Through the work of his hands he praised God and cooperated with God in feeding the world. Isidore generously shared what he harvested with others, even birds. He never hoarded what he had as the man in Jesus' parable did.

Reader: Luke 12:16–21 (The rich fool doesn't share.)

Leader: St. Isidore valued the Mass. At the Eucharist, bread made from wheat and wine made from grapes become the body and blood of Christ. The work of our hands is offered to the Father for the salvation of the world. Let us pray together the prayer the church prays at Mass on St. Isidore's feast.

All: Lord God,

    all creation is yours, and you call us to serve you

    by caring for the gifts that surround us.

    May the example of St. Isidore urge us

    to share our food with the hungry

    and to work for the salvation of mankind.

    We ask this through our Lord Jesus Christ your Son,

    who lives and reigns with you and the Holy Spirit,

    one God forever and ever. Amen.

A Maze with a Message

Find the way from the church in Madrid to the fields of Señor de Vergas. Then, starting with the second letter, circle every other letter on the path. You will see a Bible message that St. Isidore lived. Write it here: _____ _____.

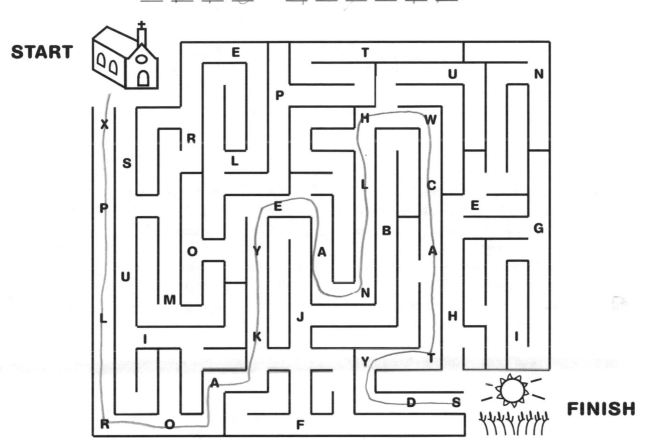

START   FINISH

Seeds of Eternal Life

On each packet of seeds write a virtue St. Isidore practiced. Then draw a plant, real or imaginary, which represents that virtue for you.

SEEDS   SEEDS

St. Anthony of Padua: Inspired Preacher

1195–June 13, 1231

Chances are that at some time in your life you have lost something and were told, "Pray to St. Anthony." This popular saint is the number one helper in finding lost objects. No one knows why this is so, although several stories are told to explain it. One story is that a woman told Anthony that she misplaced a large amount of money. Anthony directed her to go home and sweep. The woman did and found the money. Another story is that a man took Anthony's prayerbook. Anthony prayed, and the man returned it to him. While Anthony lived on earth, however, his reputation was not for being a finder but for being a marvelous preacher.

A Gifted Speaker

St. Anthony was not born in Padua but in Lisbon, Portugal, and was baptized Ferdinand. His parents were members of the nobility and had their son taught by the priests at the cathedral. When Ferdinand was fifteen, he joined the order of St. Augustine. After two years Ferdinand desired more solitude, so he was transferred to a house where he could pray and study in peace and quiet. During his eight years there he became an expert in Scripture.

Then one day in 1220 his life changed its course. The bodies of the first five Franciscan martyrs were brought to the city from Morocco, where they had been missionaries.

Ferdinand was deeply moved. He longed to be like them and give his life for Christ. Because it was unlikely that he could do this in his community, he left and joined the Franciscans. He took the name Anthony. Soon he sailed to Morocco to preach the gospel. To his dismay he became very sick and had to leave. On the way back to Europe his ship was driven off course, and he landed in Sicily. There he heard that a large meeting of all Franciscans was to take place in Assisi. Anthony went there and saw St. Francis. At the end of the meeting Anthony was assigned to a hermitage where he prayed and studied in solitude.

One day at an ordination, no one was prepared to speak. Anthony was called on to give the address spontaneously, relying on the Holy Spirit to provide the right words. Although Anthony was reluctant to do the task, he did a superb job. The head of the Franciscans promptly assigned him to preach around the country. He also made him the first Franciscan to teach theology to other Franciscans.

Although Anthony was small and somewhat stout, he had many gifts that made him a preacher who influenced many people. Anthony had a powerful voice, an extraordinary memory, knowledge of Scripture, and a sense for how to speak eloquently. He also had a very great desire to bring people to God. His holiness attracted huge crowds in Italy and France. At this time there were many heretics, people who spread false teaching. So well did Anthony present the truths of the faith in order to defend the church's teaching that he became known as the Hammer of the Heretics. To illustrate Anthony's great success as a preacher a story is told that he once preached to fish. They all stood up on their tails and listened attentively!

Anthony the Wonder Worker

Miracles were not uncommon for Anthony. They earned him the title Wonder Worker. Anthony also worked for the poor. He pleaded for them and helped release people who were in prison because of their debts.

For a time Anthony was head of the Franciscans in one region. He once visited the pope to ask questions that had come up at a meeting of the Franciscans. At that visit the pope released Anthony from his duties so that he could preach full time. From then on Anthony made his home in Padua where he was greatly loved. After a series of sermons in 1231, Anthony ran out of strength and went away to rest. Soon realizing that he did not have long to live, he asked to be taken back to Padua. Before reaching the city, he died. He was only thirty-six years old. Not even a year later he was canonized. Because he was such an outstanding teacher of the faith, in 1946 St. Anthony was named a doctor of the church.

Franciscans have a custom of giving "St. Anthony's bread" to the poor on Tuesdays, the day Anthony was buried. On this day people also pray St. Anthony's novena, prayers said for nine Tuesdays in a row. In addition to helping to find lost objects, Anthony is the patron of Portugal, marriage, childless women, the poor, harvests, travelers, miners, and animals. Many pictures and statues of Anthony show him holding the Child Jesus or a book.

What Do You Think?

- How did God lead Anthony to his ministry of preaching?
- What did Anthony do to show great love for God?
- How can you preach by your actions?
- What gifts did Anthony have? What gifts do you have?
- How did studying Scripture help Anthony?
- Where can you find good preaching?

Things to Do

1. Spend an extra ten minutes praying and reading the Bible.
2. Send money to an organization that feeds the poor.
3. Compare St. Anthony to his namesake, St. Anthony of Egypt.
4. Tell someone about St. Anthony of Padua.
5. Find Portugal, Morocco, Italy, and France on the map.
6. Draw a picture of St. Anthony preaching to fish.
7. Write a one-minute homily about God or your faith.
8. Pray to St. Anthony on Tuesdays to help you to know what God wants you to do in life.

Craft: A Bible Bookmark

Cut off one of the bottom corners of an envelope to make a triangular bookmark. Use markers to print a verse about the Bible on it and decorate it. (Suggestions: "Your word is a lamp for my path," "There's no chaining the Word of God," "Speak, Lord, I'm listening," "God's Word is living and active.") Place the marker over the corner of a page in your Bible.

God's Word Is Living & Active!

A Playlet: Anthony's in Town

Characters: Raymond, Helen, and their son James

(The family is seated around a table eating.)

Raymond: This Saturday a Franciscan is giving a talk. He's supposed to be a dynamic speaker. People call him Anthony of Padua although he was born in Lisbon, Portugal.

Helen: Is he the priest who travels from town to town explaining the faith and getting people to come to God?

Raymond: Yes. He used to be head of the Franciscans in his region, but the pope released him from that job so he could preach full time.

Helen: If I'm not mistaken, Anthony is the one Ann's husband heard speak when he was away on a business trip. Robert came back a changed man. He has started going to Mass, and Ann said he controls his temper now with her and the children. I'd like to hear Anthony.

James: Our teacher was talking about him. He said he met him when Anthony had just returned sick from Africa where he was a missionary. We get extra credit if we go to hear him, but that's the last thing I want to do on a Saturday afternoon. My friends and I have other plans.

Raymond: Young man, maybe you'd better change those plans. Think of it—someday you may be telling your children you heard the great Anthony speak. Besides, he might say something that will change your attitude, which your mother and I are beginning to worry about.

James (whining): Ah, Dad, what will my friends say?

Raymond: Why don't you talk them into coming too?

Helen: Yes. I'm sure most of the town will be there. Anthony draws such crowds that he speaks in marketplaces instead of in churches.

Raymond: Even if we end up in the back, we'll still be able to hear. They say Anthony's voice is that powerful, even though he doesn't look healthy. He's wearing himself out with a schedule that would kill a much bigger man.

Helen: This could be the chance of a lifetime. And right now I feel I need an inspiring talk about God. James, from this man's reputation, he's not going to be boring. How about it? Let's go.

Raymond: James?

James: All right. I guess I could use the extra credit.

Prayer Service

Song: "Here I Am, Lord," "Take, Lord, Receive," "All My Days," "They'll Know We Are Christians," or "We Are Many Parts"

Leader: God showered many gifts on St. Anthony. This saint used his gifts to the utmost. He did not let them rust. And he used them in the right way: to give glory to God and to help other people. The Holy Spirit has gifted all of us in different ways.

Reader: 1 Corinthians 12:4–7 (Spiritual gifts differ.)

Leader: St. Anthony discovered his gift for preaching by accident. Let us pray to learn what our gifts are and to use those gifts.

All: St. Anthony, our gifts may be hidden. Pray that we may find those special gifts God has given us.

Leader: Then pray that we use them and not let them go to waste.

All: Help us to focus all our talents and powers on showing love for God and for the other people God made and loves.

Leader: May we be proud of our gifts and thank God for them.

All: May we not envy the gifts that others have, but give thanks for them, too.

Leader: St. Anthony, help us to be devoted to God like you.

All: Then, by losing our lives to God, we will save them and enjoy eternal life. Amen.

St. Anthony's Journey

Use a penny or another small object for a marker. Roll a die. If you can state a correct fact about St. Anthony, you may go the number of spaces the die shows. See how many rolls it takes to get to the end. You might play with a partner and have a race. For variety, you could play a game stating facts about the Bible or a game stating facts about your faith.

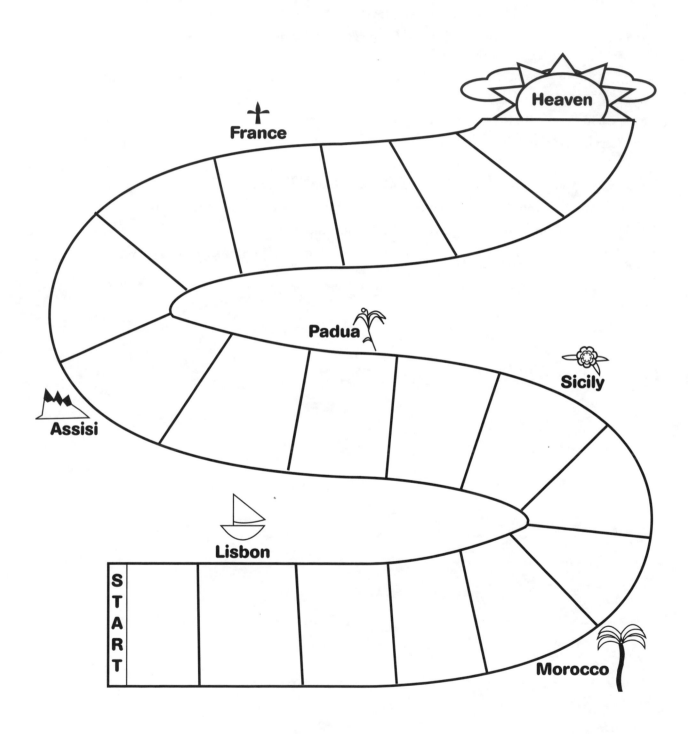

St. Ignatius Loyola: God's Soldier

1491?–July 31, 1556

God calls people in different ways. St. Paul was knocked to the ground by a bright light. In Ignatius's case, a cannonball turned his attention to God. Ignatius became the founder of the Jesuits, one of the largest groups of religious men in the world.

God's Crazy Man

Ignatius was born at the family castle at Loyola in Spain, the youngest of thirteen. His family on both sides was noble. Ignatius's mother died when he was very young, and his father died when Ignatius was sixteen. Already he had been sent to live with another noble family and be prepared for a life in court, a life of ambition and pleasure. When this family angered the royal family and lost its fortune, Ignatius went to another family and became a soldier instead.

His military career ended quickly. While Ignatius was defending the castle of Pamplona against the French, a cannonball struck his legs, breaking one and wounding the other. The broken leg was set so badly that it had to be broken again and reset two more times. These operations were very painful and left one leg shorter than the other. During his long recovery, Ignatius wanted to read. The only books available were about the life of Christ and the saints. These weren't the kind of books Ignatius was looking for, but he read them. Ignatius was so impressed by these books that he made up his mind to be a saint, too.

As soon as he was well, Ignatius made a pilgrimage to the shrine of our Lady at Montserrat.

Pledging to be Mary's knight, he placed his sword there, gave away all he owned, and put on a rough habit. For a year he stayed in the nearby town of Manresa, living with Dominicans or in a shelter for the poor. He would go to a cave to pray and do penance, and he nursed the sick in a hospital. Most important, he began his great work, the *Spiritual Exercises*, a book that guides people to pray and live for God. People called him God's crazy man.

Ignatius then went to Jerusalem by donkey and tried to convert the Muslims until he was asked to leave. The authorities were afraid he would be kidnapped.

The Society of Jesus

Ignatius returned to Spain and, at the age of thirty-three, began to study with students much younger than himself. He studied for eleven years, attending several universities. He lived as a beggar. Twice Ignatius was suspected of teaching false doctrine and was imprisoned. On being freed, he went to Paris to study. There, six other students, including St. Francis Xavier, joined him in his religious way of life. They vowed to practice poverty and chastity. They also vowed to preach the gospel in Palestine or, if this wasn't possible, to do whatever the pope asked. Two years later the group had grown to ten. A war kept them from sailing to Palestine, so they went to the pope. On the way there Ignatius had a vision of Christ carrying his cross. Christ said to him, "I will be favorable to you in Rome."

The prediction came true. The pope allowed the nine men who weren't already priests to be ordained. The men called themselves the Company of Jesus. They became a religious community named the Society of Jesus with Ignatius as their superior general, or head. Their motto was "For the greater glory of God," and they made a solemn vow of obedience to the pope. Because the Jesuits put themselves at his service, the pope assigned them ministries including giving retreats, teaching, and missionary work. They did much to reform the church.

Ignatius spent the rest of his life in Rome leading the Jesuits. He wrote the rule of life for his order as well as thousands of letters. He founded homes for orphans, catechumens, and penitent women. He also started the Roman College for Jesuits and the German College in Rome.

Although he was sick often, Ignatius died unexpectedly on July 31, 1556. By that time his order had grown to one thousand members who were all over the world. St. Ignatius was canonized in 1622. He is the patron of spiritual exercises and retreats.

What Do You Think?

- Why did Ignatius turn his life around?
- Why was obedience so important to Ignatius? When did he practice it?
- What did Ignatius do for the glory of God?
- How did Ignatius help the church?
- How can you show devotion to Mary?

Things to Do

1. Have a mini-retreat. Spend a half-hour praying and reading the Bible, perhaps on a Sunday.
2. Read a biography of a saint. List three ways you can imitate him or her.
3. Find out about the contributions of the Jesuits in the United States. Write a report.
4. Ignatius was often a pilgrim. Visit a shrine or church.
5. Research Jerusalem and the Holy Land today. Make a short travel guide with pictures.
6. Write a poem or prayer related to St. Ignatius.
7. Resolve to do some penance, especially on Fridays.
8. Renew yourself by praying a Morning Offering and giving your day to God.

Craft: Doorknob Hanger

Cut a sheet of construction paper to about nine inches by five inches. About one-half inch from the top, draw a circle about two inches wide. From the top of the paper make a slit down into this circle and cut it out. With crayons or markers print vertically, "All for the greater glory of God." Decorate the doorknob hanger and hang it on the doorknob of the room where you sleep.

All for the greater glory of God!

A Playlet: A Soldier to Follow

Characters: Francis Xavier, Peter Favre

Peter: Well, Francis, congratulations! How does it feel to have made Ignatius's Spiritual Exercises?

Francis: What a powerful spiritual tool Ignatius created at Manresa! I'm a new man. God spoke to me heart to heart during those days, thanks to Ignatius.

Peter: Your opinion of him has certainly changed. When you and I were roommates studying in Paris, you couldn't stand Ignatius.

Francis: Yes, I thought he was just a foolish old man, a disabled soldier who limped and was too thin. All his talk of holy things and religious practices drove me crazy.

Peter: You poked fun at me and his other followers until our conversations opened your eyes.

Francis: What woke me up was Ignatius's response to me. He would always ask me Christ's question in Scripture: "What does it profit a man to win the whole world and lose his soul?"

Peter: Yes, you had the world in the palm of your hand. You were athletic and handsome, and you were getting your degree. You even had your own servant.

Francis: And now look at me. I've given it all up to join Ignatius. But I don't think I've ever been happier than when the seven of us made vows. How fortunate that you were already a priest and could celebrate the Eucharist for us that day.

Peter: I wonder if we will be able to fulfill our vow of going to the Holy Land and working for the church there.

Francis: If God wills. Ignatius isn't exactly sure where God is leading us. He doesn't think he is founding a religious community. For the time being we will just have to continue our studies in theology, and trust in God.

Peter: We will live our lives of poverty and chastity consecrated to God.

Francis: And we will follow our father, Ignatius, for the glory of God.

Prayer Service

Song: "Only This I Want," "Centered in Christ," "Seek Ye First," "Take, Lord, Receive," or "Song of Jesus Christ"

Leader: St. Ignatius focused his entire life on Jesus Christ. He encouraged and inspired others to do the same. He could easily echo the words of St. Paul in Scripture:

Reader: 1 Corinthians 10:31–11:1 (Do all for the glory of God.)

Leader: Lord, like St. Ignatius may we keep you as the center of our life. May we often speak to you in prayer, make sacrifices, and try to love others as you do. May we join with St. Ignatius in saying,

All: Take, Lord, receive all my liberty, my memory, my understanding, my entire will.

Leader: You have given me all that I have, all that I am.

All: To you, Lord, I now return it. All is yours.

Leader: Give me only your love and your grace.

All: With these I am rich enough, and I have no more to ask. Amen.

Name Game

How many words can you make using the letters in the name Ignatius? List them. The letters may be used only as many times as they occur.

_____	_____	_____	_____	_____	_____
_____	_____	_____	_____	_____	_____
_____	_____	_____	_____	_____	_____
_____	_____	_____	_____	_____	_____
_____	_____	_____	_____	_____	_____

A Christian T-Shirt

On the shirt below design a saying for a Christian whose life is centered on Jesus. You might be able to copy your design onto a real shirt using permanent markers or fabric crayons.

St. Clare: Quiet Light

1193?–August 11, 1253

Friends can help each other grow closer to God. Two of the most famous friends in the history of the church are St. Clare and St. Francis of Assisi. He founded the Franciscans; she founded the first Franciscan community for women. Today Franciscans pray and work throughout the world.

Clare and Francis

Clare belonged to a wealthy and noble family in Assisi. When she was a young girl, she heard St. Francis speak. He had once been a leader among the town's well-to-do young men, a group whose main goal in life was to have a good time. Now he was completely changed. Francis went about as a beggar, preaching about the love of God. While others saw Francis as a man who had lost his mind, Clare saw him as someone who held the key to peace, joy, and eternal life. Clare was so fascinated by St. Francis and his way of life, that she decided to imitate him.

On Palm Sunday, when Clare was eighteen years old, a strange thing happened. At the distribution of palms, the bishop himself came to her and handed her a palm. That night she and a companion secretly left the family castle. They went about a mile to the Portiuncula where Francis and his men lived. There at the chapel of Our Lady of the Angels, she met St. Francis and his brothers. He cut off her long, blond hair and gave her a rough robe to wear. He took her to stay at a Benedictine convent. Clare's family was very upset and became even more upset when her fifteen-year-old sister Agnes joined her days later. St. Francis

gave them a rule, and they became a Second Order of Franciscans. Eventually Clare's mother and another sister would join as well.

A Strict Way of Life

Soon Clare and her sisters moved into a small house next to San Damiano church. That was where St. Francis had first heard God's call to rebuild the church. They lived a very hard life to show their love of God. They went barefoot, slept on the ground, and ate no meat. They lived in silence and did not leave the convent, except to beg for food. Because they wanted to be poor, the sisters ate only what was donated to them and owned no property. Once when the sisters' rule, or written way of life, was being formed, the pope tried to allow the sisters to own property. Clare resisted and won. However, she did have to modify some aspects of her strict way of life. As she came to realize, "Our bodies are not made of brass."

St. Francis made Clare the abbess when she was twenty-one, and for forty-one years she served as head of the community. She did not give herself privileges, though. She took care of the sick sisters, served the sisters at table, and even washed the feet of the begging sisters when they came home. Church officials often came to consult Clare. St. Francis remained her good friend. When he was undergoing treatment for his blindness, he stayed at San Damiano and Clare cared for him.

Clare's Powers of Prayer

St. Clare was very prayerful. It was said that after she prayed, her face became bright with dazzling light. Her prayer was powerful. Twice an enemy army of invading Saracens was close to attacking the convent. St. Clare had the Blessed Sacrament set at the convent gate and prayed. Both times the convent was spared. Clare told her sisters that God saved them because of their devotion to the Blessed Sacrament.

There is also a story that one Christmas Eve Clare was sick in bed, but was able to see the services in the chapel just as though she were there. For this reason Clare has been named the patron of television and of people who have problems with their vision.

For twenty-seven years St. Clare was sick and often in bed. She bore this cross without complaining. The pope visited her twice near the end of her life. On August 11, 1253, Clare died at the age of sixty-one. Her last words were, "Blessed be you, my God, for having created me." In 1255 she was canonized. Her body remains incorrupt. Today the Franciscan sisters who live her rule are called the Poor Clares. In art, St. Clare often holds a lily.

What Do You Think?

- Why do you think Clare became a sister?
- What did Clare give up for God?
- What made the Saracens turn back from the convent?
- What penances or sacrifices can you make for God?
- How can you influence your friends to love God more?

Things to Do

1. Write a newspaper article that might have appeared in the *Assisi Herald* after Clare joined Francis.

2. Do without something that is not a need. Make your sacrifice for the intention of the relief of the poor in your city or town. If possible, donate to them the money saved by your sacrifice.

3. Try to make a visit to the Blessed Sacrament or participate in eucharistic devotions at your parish.

4. Keep track of how many hours of television you watch during one week. Reflect on whether your time was well spent and what you could have done instead.

5. Keep track of which television shows you watch during one week and consider whether they were the kind that God would approve of.

6. Find out about the Poor Clares today.

7. Compose a prayer thanking God for the gift of sight.

8. Clare shared Francis's love for creation. Make a collage of beautiful nature photos.

Craft: Lily

Turn an 8 1/2 x 11-inch piece of paper, so that the shorter sides are at the top and bottom. Place a dot 8 1/2 inches up from the bottom of the right side. Draw a line from the bottom left corner to the dot and cut along the line to make a triangle. Fold this triangle in half and hold it so that the longest side is at the top. Place a dot along the top of the triangle, three inches from the right point. Draw a line from this dot to the bottom point of the triangle and fold the paper along this line. Fold the left hand side of the triangle so that the edge lines up with the right edge of the paper. Turn the paper over. Place a dot three inches from the bottom point on the right and left edges. Place another dot half way along the top horizontal edge. Draw lines from the dots on both side edges to the dot on the top edge to form an upside-down *V*. Cut along the lines and discard the top of the paper. Open the remaining paper and tape the two edges of the lily together around a green pipe cleaner or doubled strip of green construction paper. Starting at the bottom of each petal, pull the paper between your thumb and a scissor blade to curl it outward. From yellow construction paper, cut three four-inch strips with small knobs on the end. Glue or tape the bottom of these strips inside the lily (they should be slightly taller than the lily). Add leaves to the stem if desired.

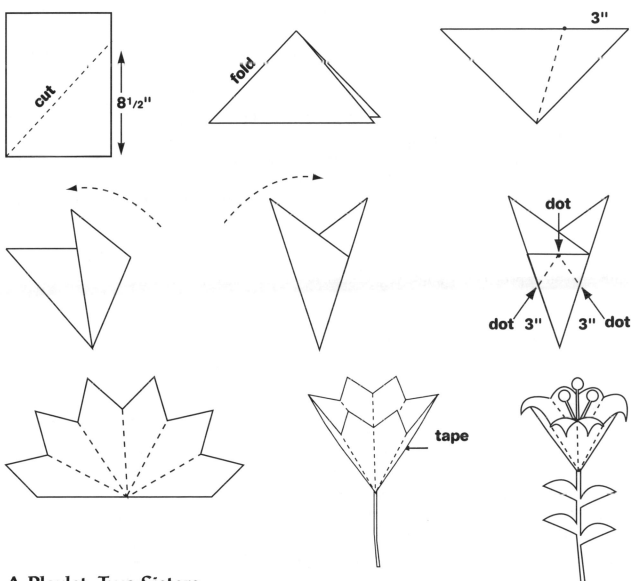

A Playlet: Two Sisters

Characters: St. Clare, Agnes

(Clare is standing. Agnes enters.)

Clare: Agnes, you came!

Agnes: Wait until mother and father discover I'm gone. They haven't gotten over your escape two weeks ago.

Clare: I feel bad about that. We must trust our Lord's words that everyone who has given up houses or brothers or sisters or father or mother or children or lands for the sake of his name will receive a hundred times more and inherit eternal life.

Agnes: Just think, we have traded a boring life as ladies of luxury for the exciting life of beggars!

Clare: Francis and his men aren't the only ones who can have the adventure of living totally dependent on God.

Agnes: I remember when you first heard Francis talk. You came home so full of joy I thought you would burst.

Clare: Because everything Francis said echoed what my heart felt. His words drew me to God and made me want to live for God alone.

Agnes: I love the way Francis finds God in creation. It reminds me of the way we used to speak on our picnics when we were young.

Clare: *Were* young!? I'm only nineteen, and you are four years younger!

Agnes: Isn't it wonderful? We have practically our whole lives yet to pray and give glory to God.

Clare: And it looks as if we'll be spending them at San Damiano. There's a house near the church where Francis is planning for us to live. The Benedictines and these other sisters have been kind to me since I came, but our way of life as members of Francis's second order will be quite different. We won't own any land, and we'll beg for our food. To do penance for the world we'll go barefoot and sleep on the ground.

Agnes: Clare, we're like pioneers, aren't we?

Clare: Right, we're marking out a path that perhaps someday many other women will follow. Although other people may think we are out of our minds, I'm convinced we're doing what God wants.

Agnes: Like Francis.

Clare: Yes, like Francis.

Prayer Service

Song: "Trust in the Lord," "Only in God," "Be Not Afraid," or "Seek the Lord"

Leader: Clare had courage because she trusted in God. She trusted when she left home to follow Francis. She relied on God to save her convent from the enemy army. She praised God throughout her long years of suffering. In Scripture God encourages us to trust him.

Reader: Isaiah 43:1–4 (God tells us to trust in his love.)

Leader: Let us ask Clare to pray that we have a strong faith like hers.

All: St. Clare, you risked everything to follow Francis and live for God alone.

Leader: Pray that we may be brave enough to do what God wants, especially when we cannot see how things will work out.

All: When we are threatened by enemies, pray that we may depend on God to save us.

Leader: When we are faced with sorrows and sufferings, pray that we may trust that God will work out everything for the good.

All: Then one day may we be with you praising God in heaven. Amen.

Life with God

Color yellow or shade with pencil the shapes that contain words related to St. Clare. You will see something she treasured.

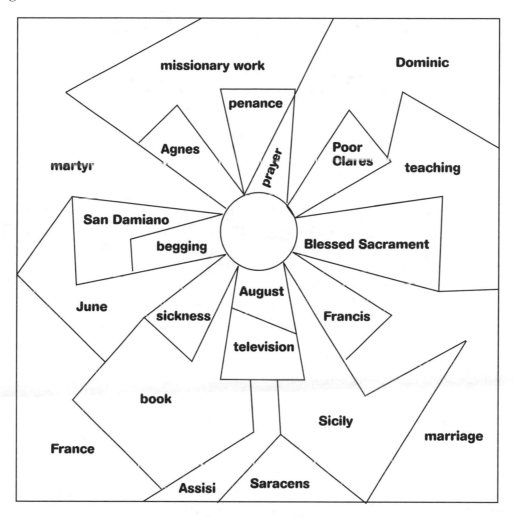

Glory to God!

In the box draw something in nature that you like. Write a short prayer of praise to God for this object on the lines.

St. Vincent de Paul: Apostle of Charity

April 24, 1581–September 27, 1660

D oes your parish or neighborhood have a St. Vincent de Paul Society? This organization that works for the poor takes its name from a man whose life was devoted to the poor. St. Vincent de Paul is known for persuading the rich people of France to be rich in good works. He was short and had a large nose and large ears, but his twinkling eyes, charm, and humility helped him accomplish many things. His accomplishments, though, were far different from the goals he had set as a young priest.

Champion of the Poor

Vincent was born to a peasant family in France. He had several brothers and sisters. As a boy Vincent tended sheep, pigs, and other animals. His father sent him to study to be a priest, and he was ordained when he was only nineteen. He studied theology for four more years. Vincent planned to live a comfortable life as many priests at that time did. He would celebrate the sacraments and receive the income of a nearby abbey. If he were lucky, his income would be large. God, however, had other plans for him.

A woman left Vincent some money that a young man owed her. Vincent traveled to collect this debt and while sailing back was captured by pirates and made a slave. He was sold several times—once to a fisherman, another time to a Muslim alchemist—and finally escaped. He went to Paris where he shared an apartment with a government official. One day when Vincent was ill, the man who delivered his medicine stole a purse. Vincent was accused of the theft. Until the culprit confessed six months later, this accusation hung over Vincent's head as he looked for a job.

In Paris, Vincent had met a holy priest named Pierre Bérulle whom he trusted to guide his life. Perhaps through him Vincent was appointed to distribute alms for Queen Marguerite, who had been King Henry IV's wife before their marriage was annulled. It looked as if Vincent was on his way to becoming a fashionable, wealthy priest. During this time he had strong temptations against the faith. These disappeared, however, when Vincent decided to give himself entirely to working for the poor.

To test him, Bérulle arranged to have Vincent be pastor of a church in a poor village. There Vincent was happy and successful until Bérulle directed him to a new role: chaplain and tutor to the noble Gondi family. The Countess de Gondi, named Marguerite, also made Vincent her spiritual guide. Uncomfortable with high society, Vincent left the Gondis. Bérulle sent him to another parish where the people were not very religious. Vincent led many people back to the faith and Christian living, including a count who was a famous bully dedicated to dueling.

At this parish Vincent once preached about a family whose members were poor and sick. People donated so much to the family that food was wasted. Vincent saw that charity needed to be organized. He formed the first Confraternity of Charity. The members prepared and brought food to the poor. They also prepared the people for the sacraments and for death.

A Return to the Gondis

Eventually, Marguerite and friends of Vincent persuaded him to return to the Gondis. On the family's estates were seven or eight thousand workers. Both Vincent and Marguerite were concerned for their spiritual life. One day when Vincent was at the bedside of a dying peasant, he realized how much these poor people needed to know God and the faith.

Vincent conducted missions and established more Confraternities of Charity, to bring food, clothing, and medicine to the poor. Those in the women's groups were called Ladies of Charity. Donations were collected from the rich and spent directly for the poor. Marguerite and her sister-in-law supported the work by generous donations and by helping with their own hands. Queen Anne of Austria was president of one group.

Fifteen years later Vincent de Paul began the Daughters of Charity, country girls who helped the wealthy, high-born Ladies of Charity in practical matters. St. Louise de Marillac was his right hand. She found the girls and trained them, taking a group of them into her house. Vincent regarded these girls as members of a lay association, not as nuns. He told them, "Your monasteries are the houses of the sick; your cell is a hired room; your chapel, the parish church; your cloister, the streets of the city." They soon became known as sisters, but they renewed their vows each year. Vincent had weekly conferences with them in Paris.

The Count de Gondi was the General of the Galleys. In those days ships were powered by prisoners and slaves who rowed in the galleys below. These men lived and worked in terrible conditions. Vincent de Paul helped them so much that a legend arose that he took the place of one slave who had a family.

New Responsibilities

As if he didn't have enough to do, Vincent was given a new responsibility. When St. Francis de Sales and St. Jane Frances de Chantal established houses of their Visitation community in Paris, St. Vincent became their superior.

Before long St. Vincent de Paul had his own community to direct. The Gondis contributed large sums of money to fund rural missions. When Vincent could not find a religious community to carry on this work, he assumed the task. Others joined him, and a new congregation came into being, the Congregation of the Mission, now known as the Vincentians. They were offered the Priory of Saint-Lazare to live in.

Not all priests in France were as zealous as Vincent. In fact, many of them needed to be reformed. At the suggestion of a bishop, Vincent began instructing seminarians. In return for Saint-Lazare, the Archbishop of Paris required that seminarians be given a two-week retreat there before being ordained. Vincent opened his own seminaries. Soon his community was in charge of fifty-three major seminaries in France. Vincent also held Tuesday conferences for a select group of priests and gave retreats for laymen and priests.

Vincent greatly influenced the church in France in another way. He advised the king in spiritual matters. Anne of Austria saw that Vincent was present at the deathbed of King Louis XIII. She then set up a committee for church affairs and appointed Vincent a member against his wishes.

St. Vincent was responsible for many other good works. During war he and his communities raised vast sums of money to help the victims. He ransomed more than 1200 galley slaves. He sent his Fathers to other countries as missionaries. His Daughters of Charity opened schools for peasant girls. He opened a large house for beggars, orphanages, an asylum for the mentally ill, and a hospital for foundlings.

After a long illness, Vincent died at the age of eighty. God's grace had transformed this man who had once been a snob and a grouch into a loving person. Once known to all as Monsieur Vincent, he is now called St. Vincent. It is no surprise that he is the patron of charitable organizations.

What Do You Think?

• Why do you think St. Vincent had such a heart for the poor?

• Who were some people that influenced St. Vincent? How did he influence others?

• How can you influence your friends to do good?

• What makes the life of a priest difficult?

• How did St. Vincent manage to do so much for God in his lifetime?

• How can you share what you have with others?

Things to Do

1. Find out what the corporal and spiritual works of mercy are. Choose one and illustrate it.

2. With family members or classmates act out the parable of the Good Samaritan found in Luke 10:25–37.

3. Report on the work of the St. Vincent de Paul Society and its founder Frederic Ozanam.

4. Plan a way that you can help the poor and sick.

5. Resolve to serve others.

6. Research the life of St. Louise de Marillac, St. Frances de Sales, or St. Jane Frances de Chantal.

Craft: Coat of Arms

Design a coat of arms for St. Vincent. Draw the shape of a coat of arms and divide it into four sections. In each section draw a symbol representing St. Vincent and his life. Draw a bar along the bottom and in it letter a motto or a keyword for him. Cut out the coat of arms and staple or tape it to a sheet of different colored construction paper so that it stands out.

Vincent de Paul

A Playlet: A Holy Director

Characters: St. Francis de Sales, St. Jane Frances de Chantal

(Francis and Jane are seated.)

Jane: I'm delighted that we are allowed to choose directors for our new Visitation community.

Francis: For our houses in Paris, there is only one person I would entrust with the job.

Jane: I know—Monsieur Vincent. He's such a good man, always a gentleman, even though he always tells people, "I'm nothing but a swineherd." But how can we even think of asking him when he is so busy? He still organizes missions for the country districts and conducts them himself. This is in addition to organizing the Confraternities of Charity for men and women. Those groups are blossoming all over.

Francis: I know. What a splendid plan to have the rich assume their responsibility to share their goods with the poor! Leave it to Vincent to carry out such a scheme. His love for others is contagious.

Jane: Now he is also the chaplain of the galley slaves. Those poor men live in such wretched conditions that they die like flies. Vincent sees to their spiritual needs and helps them deal with their lot in life. I don't know how he will have time to oversee our houses.

Francis: Well, you know the saying, "If you want something done, ask a busy person."

Jane: We might have to wait awhile for a response. Vincent takes forever to move on things. He lives by his words, "You should not tread on the heels of Providence."

Francis: Yes, however, the rest of the saying is: "But if Providence opens the way, you should run." You and I have to suggest to Vincent that God is inviting him to run our way. If we have to wait, it will be worth it. Vincent has the holiness and the common sense the sisters need to guide them in this crucial beginning stage.

Jane: And he seems to like tackling new projects. Although he moves slowly, Vincent accomplishes an incredible amount. We should at least ask him to consider helping us with our Visitation convents.

Francis: Let's do it together. I've invited him to dinner Wednesday to discuss a few passages in my book on spirituality. Why don't you come too, and we'll persuade him over a delicious meal.

Jane: Good idea. Who knows what else Vincent will undertake for God's kingdom during his lifetime?

Prayer Service

Song: "Service," "Whatsoever You Do," "Jesu, Jesu, Fill Us with Your Love," "They'll Know We Are Christians by Our Love," or "A New Commandment"

Leader: To be a Christian is to serve. St. Vincent knew this and he joyfully served everyone, especially the poor and sick. In this way he followed Christ who healed the sick, taught the ignorant, and even washed the feet of his apostles.

Reader: John 13:4–5, 12–15 (Jesus washes the apostles' feet.)

Leader: Let us ask St. Vincent to give us hearts that are filled with compassion for others, Christian hearts.

All: St. Vincent de Paul, please pray for us that we may be loving people.

Leader: Pray that we may hear the cries of the poor and answer them.

All: Pray that we may do what we can for other brothers and sisters who are hungry and sick.

Leader: Let us take time from our busy lives to work to better their lives.

All: Let us open our hands generously to share our blessings. Let us open our hearts to show them the love of Jesus. Amen.

Wheel of Fortune

Finish the motto of St. Vincent de Paul's Confraternities of Charity, which is the secret of true wealth. Starting with FO, write the letters in every other box on the lines, going twice around the wheel. Divide the letters into words.

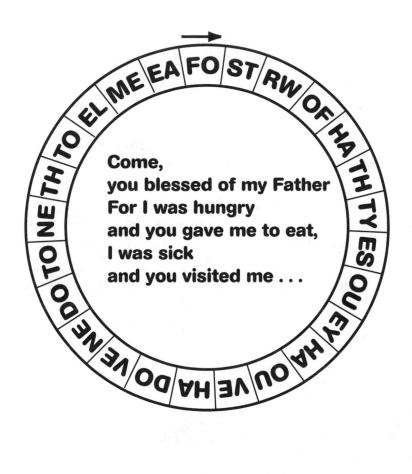

Come,
you blessed of my Father
For I was hungry
and you gave me to eat,
I was sick
and you visited me . . .

_____

_____

A Helping Hand

Trace your hand in the box below. For each finger write a good deed you will do this week.

I will clean my room.

I will walk the dog.

I will wash the dishes.

I will help Mom cook.

I will help Dad with yardwork.

St. Francis of Assisi: Knight for Peace

1181?–October 3, 1226

If you had lived in Assisi, Italy in the early thirteenth century, you would know all about Francis of Assisi. He was the talk of the town. This son of the rich cloth merchant Pietro Bernadone had chosen to be a beggar! You would often see Francis, clothed in a peasant's robe with a rope tied around his waist, begging in the streets. Like others, you would probably think he had lost his mind. You would not realize that in that disguise was a true knight—a knight of God.

Serving Lady Poverty

Francis had not been religious as a young man. He and his friends partied until all hours of the night with good food and wine, and the Assisi streets rang with their noise and their singing. He dreamed of being a knight and winning wars in the name of a fair lady. When Assisi went to war, Francis actually did become a soldier. His dream-come-true, however, was more like a nightmare: Francis was captured and spent a year in prison, where he became sick.

After this experience, Francis realized that he was really called to be a knight for God. The lady he was to serve was Lady Poverty. In other words, he was to live as a poor man. Francis began to change. He gave things from his father's house to the poor, and he no longer avoided lepers. One day he met a leper on the road. Instead of just tossing the poor man a bag of coins, Francis gave it to him and kissed his hands. He began to care for lepers in their hospitals.

But what exactly was Francis to do as a knight of God? He prayed and waited for direction. Then one day God spoke. Francis was praying before the crucifix in the church of San Damiano (St. Damian's). He heard God say, "Go, Francis, and repair my house, for it is falling down."

Francis took these words to mean he should repair churches. Obediently, he began to rebuild crumbling San Damiano's with stones and mortar. In order to get materials, he sang for stones in town. He also helped himself to some of his father's cloth and sold it. Bernardone, already embarrassed by his son's strange behavior, was furious. He had Francis taken before the bishop of Assisi, who acted as judge. When Bernardone demanded his money back, Francis removed all his clothes and laid them with some money at his father's feet. He said, "I return these clothes and money. From now on I will not call Pietro Bernardone father. I will say, 'Our Father who art in heaven.'"

Francis and His Little Brothers

From that time on Francis begged for food. He lived as a hermit until one day at Mass he learned what he was to do. The gospel that day was about Jesus instructing the apostles to go out and preach. They were to have only one robe and no sandals or staff. Francis heard this as if Jesus were talking directly to him. He put on a peasant's robe and went into town barefoot. There he spoke to crowds of people about loving God and about peace. His words touched their hearts.

Soon other men joined Francis in his way of life. He called his group Friars Minor, which means "little brothers." They were to serve others and to be little, or unimportant. They were to beg for food as they preached. Just as in his youth Francis had led men to fun and good times, he now led not only men, but also women, to the joy that lasts forever. Clare was an eighteen-year-old from a well-to-do family. She was stirred by Francis's words and drawn to live for God as he did. One night she ran away from home to Francis. Dressed as a bride, she let him cut off her long, blond curls. She put on a rough robe like his and a veil. The first convent for Clare and other Franciscan sisters was at San Damiano.

A Love of Creation

What attracted people to Francis then and still attracts them today? As God's knight, he had a great love for God's creation. He called created things sister and brother. They reminded him of God. Francis's favorite creation was the brilliant, mysterious Brother Sun. He composed a song called the "Canticle of the Sun." In it he called on created things to praise God. Because Francis loved creation, he cared for it. He pleaded with King Ferdinand II of Germany to protect certain birds. When he saw an earthworm on the road, he moved it to safety. It is said that one day he preached to a flock of many kinds of birds saying, "My sister birds, you ought to praise and thank God because you can fly, you have colorful coats, food, trees to make nests in, and beautiful voices." In response, all the birds began singing, bowing, and fluttering their wings. Then Francis blessed them.

Creatures sensed that Francis loved them. It is said that once he asked some swallows to be quiet so he could preach—and they were! Another story is about a wolf that terrorized the town of Gubbio and ate its livestock. Francis bravely went out and scolded him.

Instead of eating Francis, Brother Wolf lay down at his feet as meek as a lamb. He gave Francis his right paw as a sign that he agreed not to harm the people if they would feed him. Brother Wolf became the town pet.

God's Knight

Francis was especially brave when it came to telling people about God. At a time when Christians and Muslims were fighting, Francis went to Egypt to visit the sultan, a Muslim chief. Francis wanted to make peace and to tell him about Christ. The sultan was so impressed by Francis's courage and gentleness that he did not kill him.

Francis risked his life for Jesus because Jesus meant everything to him. It was Francis who popularized the tradition of nativity scenes in honor of Jesus' birth. In the town of Grecchio he asked to have a manger with straw set up in the woods and animals brought there. On Christmas Eve night, people gathered around the manger. Francis sang the Christmas gospel and spoke about the Prince of Peace who came as a poor child to save us.

As God's knight, Francis had the mission to repair Christ's church. This mission was confirmed in Rome. When Francis and his ragtag band of men walked there to get official approval for their community, they were not welcomed. But it is said that the pope then had a strange dream. In it he saw St. John Lateran church in Rome shaking, cracking, and ready to keel over. He then saw a little man in peasant clothes walk over to one of the leaning walls and push until the church was straight and steady again. As a result of this dream, the pope blessed Francis and his way of life. Francis and his followers went on to rebuild the church—but not with stones and mortar as he first thought. By their joy, peace, and wholehearted love of God they renewed the people of God, the living stones of the church.

Near the end of his life Francis lived like a hermit on Mount Alverna. There he was blessed with a special spiritual gift that made him more like Jesus by sharing in his suffering. He received the *stigmata*, the five wounds of Christ that sometimes miraculously appear on a person. Francis also suffered from a painful blindness. While being treated for this, he stayed at the convent of San Damiano where Clare lived. Even in his suffering he was a knight of peace. The mayor and bishop of Assisi were fighting, but when Francis arrived, they made up.

By the time Francis was forty-four his body, which he called Brother Donkey, was worn out. As Francis was dying, he asked his Franciscan brothers to lay him on the ground. There, close to the earth he loved, Francis met Sister Death. He died singing Psalm 141. Only two years later Francis, the poor little man, became a canonized saint. He had served his Lord and God well. St. Francis is the patron saint of Italy along with St. Catherine of Siena.

What Do You Think?

- Why were people attracted to St. Francis?
- Do you know anyone who is like St. Francis?
- In what way could you be like St. Francis and show peace? Joy? Love? A spirit of poverty? Love for creation?
- How can you grow in love for Jesus?
- If St. Francis could speak to us today, what would his message be?

Things to Do

1. Find out more about Franciscans. Where are they located? What do they do? What are Third Order Franciscans? Who are some famous Franciscans?
2. Paint a picture of your favorite things of creation.
3. Collect your extra clothes or toys and games and donate them to the poor.
4. Take a walk and in your heart praise God for the gifts you see and hear.
5. Find the book *Fioretti*, or *Flowers of St. Francis*, and read some of the stories about St. Francis.
6. If your parish does not hold the blessing of animals on the feast of St. Francis, try to introduce this custom.
7. Resolve to keep Jesus at the center of your life by praying morning and night prayers.

Craft: Bird

Make a paper bird to remind you of St. Francis. On a sheet of paper draw and cut out the body. Cut a horizontal slit in the middle. Accordion-pleat another sheet of paper and insert it into the slit for wings. Pull open the wings and join them over the bird with tape or a staple. Punch a hole in the wings and loop yarn through them so that the bird can hang.

A Playlet: A Walk with St. Francis

Characters: Francis, Junipero, Bernard, Louis

(The four men are walking along together.)

Junipero: That was really a generous town, wasn't it? We were given enough bread for at least five meals.

Francis: Yes, we can take some to the lepers.

Bernard: Did you notice that tall man in the crowd, Father Francis? When you spoke about being at peace with oneself, he listened so intently. There were tears in his eyes.

Francis: Yes, that was Carlos. He'll be joining us shortly as a Friar Minor. God is blessing us with more and more men, just as Sister Clare is being blessed with more and more women. Soon we'll be able to go out to other countries to spread the news of God's love.

Junipero: Did you ever think you would be preaching like this, Francis?

Francis: Certainly not when I was roaming the streets of Assisi with the other teenage boys. Even when God first called me, I thought my life's work was to build churches. Remember how you helped me?

Junipero: Yes, my muscles and bones will never forget.

Louis: Speaking of God, look at that sun. I've never seen such a gorgeous sunset.

Francis: If Brother Sun is so brilliant and wonderful, imagine how much more so must be his creator. How privileged we are to be in God's service. Brother Junipero, are you happy?

Junipero: Of course, Father Francis. I may not sing when I'm happy as you do, but I am full of joy. Who wouldn't be, in my situation? I don't own anything to worry about.

Bernard: We are as carefree as that worm over there.

Francis: Ah, Brother Worm must be lost. Let's move him off the road before someone crushes him underfoot. **(Moves worm.)** There. Now, Brother Worm, you may crawl around safely, enriching the soil for us and praising God.

Louis: If Brother Worm could talk, what do you think he would say?

Bernard: He'd probably tell us to be lowly and humble as he is. What do you think, Francis?

Francis: He'd probably pray, "My God and my all!"

Junipero: That's your prayer, Francis.

Francis: So it is. So it is.

Prayer Service

Song: "Canticle of the Sun," "All Creatures of Our God and King," or another hymn that refers to nature

Leader: God, we thank you for giving us St. Francis to show us the way to true joy. He loved your gifts of creation which led him to praise you. He depended on you as his loving Father. He followed your advice in the Bible.

Reader: Matthew 6:26–33 (The God who cares for the birds and flowers will care for you.)

Leader: By living the gospel and being like Jesus, St. Francis helped thousands of people. Lord, with your grace we can imitate him. We too can bring peace and love to the world. We pray together a prayer known as the prayer of St. Francis.

All: Lord, make me an instrument of your peace.

Where there is hatred, let me sow love;

where there is injury, pardon;

where there is doubt, faith;

where there is despair, hope;

where there is darkness, light;

where there is sadness, joy.

O Divine Master,

grant that I may not so much seek to be consoled as to console;

to be understood as to understand;

to be loved as to love;

for it is in giving that we receive;

it is in pardoning that we are pardoned,

and it is in dying that we are born to eternal life.

A Prayer

To find a favorite prayer of St. Francis, above each letter below write the letter that comes before it in the alphabet.

_____

N Z   H P E   B O E   N Z   B M M

A Crossword Puzzle

ACROSS

2. Animal Francis tamed
3. Sick persons Francis cared for
6. What the Friars Minor were supposed to be
8. Marks that let Francis share Jesus' suffering
10. Mount where Francis lived as a hermit
11. One whom Francis claimed as father
12. Person Francis loved most
13. What Francis had for God and creatures
15. Person who began Nativity scenes
18. What Francis was to repair

DOWN

1. Lady whom Francis served as a knight
4. First Franciscan sister
5. Creatures Francis preached to
7. Country Francis is patron of
9. What Francis preached and helped bring about
10. Town where Francis lived
12. What Francis's way of life leads to
14. Francis's favorite created thing that reminded him of God
16. What Francis's father sold
17. One whom Francis tried to be like

St. Martin de Porres: Father of Charity

December 9, 1579–November 3, 1639

Justice means giving all people what is due to them. It means defending their rights to such things as food, clothing, and shelter. How fitting it is that St. Martin de Porres is the patron of social justice. Not only did he work to help the poor, but he was poor himself. Not only did he serve groups of people who were looked down on, but he himself was the victim of prejudice.

Brother Broom

Martin was born in Lima, Peru in 1579. His father was John de Porres, a Spanish nobleman who became the governor of Panama. His mother was Anna Velazquez, a black woman. When Martin's father saw his son's dark skin, he rejected Martin as his son and left the family. He returned only for a short time. Martin had a sister Joan two years younger than he. Martin's mother was left to raise her children alone and with hardly any money. We can't blame her for being angry when she sent Martin to buy food and he came back empty-handed. He often gave their money to someone poorer than they were.

When he was twelve Martin was sent to learn the trade of a barber. In those days barbers were also doctors. Martin became known as a very good doctor. He took care of the poor and refused any payment. He could do this because at this time his father had begun supporting his family. When Martin wasn't work-ing, he was either at Mass daily or in his room praying and reading from spiritual books.

To the dismay of his patients, Martin entered the Dominican monastery of the Holy Rosary as a lay helper. His father asked the superior to make Martin at least a lay brother if not a priest, but Martin resisted. He was a humble man. This was also shown by the gentle way he bore the insults of some community members who resented having a black man in their community.

As a lay helper Martin did manual work. He cleaned the large house and worked on the farm. He was seen sweeping so often that he was called Brother Broom. Gradually Martin took on other duties. He became the barber for the three hundred men in the monastery and also their doctor. Despite his busy work schedule, Martin prayed often. When his hands weren't at work, they were holding the rosary. At night he spent hours in prayer, usually before the Blessed Sacrament.

Martin's Special Gifts

Martin gave his whole life to God. In return God gave Martin spiritual gifts. Sometimes as he prayed, Martin was raised above the ground and experienced ecstasy, a kind of holy trance. Sometimes he was invisible. Martin also had the gift of being in two places at the same time. Although he never left Lima, he was seen teaching religion to children in

China and Japan and meeting the needs of some Christians who were imprisoned in Algeria. Once when his sister Joan told how Martin had settled a heated argument between her and her husband at their house, members of his community insisted that Martin had been in the monastery all day. Before long, priests were asking his advice in spiritual matters, and novices were sent to him for instruction. Even government leaders sought his counsel. Martin's knowledge of God was learned in prayer.

Martin is most known for his gift of healing. Sometimes he would cover up his miraculous powers by pretending that some sugar water or herb had done the work. He could sense when someone in the monastery infirmary needed him. At those times even locked doors wouldn't stop him. Martin somehow knew what the sick had a craving for and would provide it. His patients were comforted just by his presence and his smile. During an epidemic that attacked sixty men at the monastery, Martin nursed them night and day. When he had too many poor patients to be taken into the monastery, Martin persuaded his sister Joan to turn her house into a hospital. One time Martin was sent to the archbishop of Mexico who was very sick. The archbishop had Martin put his hand on the side of his chest. Immediately the pain left. Martin returned to the monastery and began cleaning toilets. One of the priests saw him and asked, "Wouldn't you be better off in the archbish-op's palace?" Martin replied, "I have chosen to be a lowly thing in the house of God."

Martin cared for animals too. There is a famous story about Martin and some mice who were nibbling holes in the monastery linens. Martin caught one mouse and promised that if the mice would move to the garden, he would feed them every day. The mouse led his many friends out of the monastery, and Martin kept his promise.

Becoming a Brother

After nine years of seeing how good and holy Martin was, the Dominicans invited him to become a brother, and this time Martin agreed. He made religious vows.

Martin lived as a poor religious. His clothing was secondhand, and he had only one habit. His room was the infirmary supply room where he had a bed of planks covered by a mat. Although he himself was poor, Martin became in charge of distributing large amounts of money. People knew their donations to him would go to a worthy cause. St. Martin began Holy Cross orphanage and school. He also provided dowries, which is money required of a woman in order to be married. Every night at the monastery door he distributed food to the poor, including dogs and cats. He was called the father of the poor.

St. Martin de Porres died at the age of sixty. He is known as the patron of social justice and continues his work of healing people on earth who pray to him.

What Do You Think?

- How did Martin have a difficult childhood?
- Why did Martin become a lay helper at Holy Rosary monastery?
- What were Martin's outstanding virtues?
- How did Martin use his gift of healing?
- If Martin were living on earth today, where would you find him?
- What can you learn from the way St. Martin lived his life, especially from the way that he handled prejudice?

Things to Do

1. Visit, call, or write to someone who is sick.

2. Do something kind for an animal.

3. Spend an extra five minutes in prayer today.

4. Give some of your personal money to an organization that works for the poor.

5. Make a list of qualities that good doctors and nurses need. Write a prayer for them.

6. Discuss with a classmate racial prejudice in your country. What can you do about it?

7. Find a newspaper or magazine article about a situation that calls for justice. Make this situation the focus of your prayers for a week.

8. Make a stained-glass picture of St. Martin. Using a pencil, draw him in a black Dominican robe. Add symbols of his life such as a cross, a broom, a mouse, a dog, or a poor child. Draw curved or straight lines over the picture. Go over these lines with black crayon or marker, making them one-fourth of an inch thick. Then color the picture.

Craft: St. Martin's Broom

Tiny brooms are distributed in Peru as a sign of devotion to St. Martin. Make a broom out of construction paper. Take a two-inch square of yellow paper and cut fringe along the bottom, up to one-half of an inch from the top. Take a strip of brown paper three inches by five inches and roll up the long side to make a stick. Tape it together. Place the yellow piece an inch from the bottom of the stick and wrap it around the stick. Tape the yellow paper to the stick. If you wish, punch a hole in the top of the stick and thread it with string or yarn so that the broom can be hung.

A Playlet: Martin, a Brother?

Characters: Superior, Assistant, Novice Director

(The Superior, Assistant, and Novice Director are seated around a table.)

Superior: At this meeting I would like to propose that we have Martin de Porres make vows as a brother. He has been with us as a member of the third order for nine years now, and no one equals his holiness.

Assistant: You're right about that. Even if he didn't have special gifts like healing people and levitating during prayer, he would still seem like a saint. His humility is outstanding.

Novice Director: When prejudiced priests have treated him badly, he showed them nothing but love.

Assistant: He has always been content to do the lowliest tasks. And he does them well and with enthusiasm. Why else would he get the nickname Brother Broom?

Superior: His gift of healing could easily go to his head, but instead he tries to cover up his special powers.

Assistant: Yes, when I had a fever last month, Martin talked as if some herbs cured me. I'm sure it was just his hand on my forehead that chased the fever away so quickly.

Novice Director: If it's a question of spiritual knowledge, Martin may not have theology courses, but he is an expert in faith. You know how I send the novices to Martin in hopes that they will learn from him.

Superior: As for his love of neighbor, Martin has a heart for the poor. He can hardly wait each night to dole out the food to the poor at the gates. The other day he even gave a beggar his hat, not that that was such a prize. Martin's clothes are always secondhand.

Novice Director: And don't forget his love for the sick. The people and animals he takes in threaten to overrun our house sometimes.

Assistant: When you think about it, Martin is already living the life of a brother. He prays, lives the vows, and serves the poor. We might as well make it official.

Novice Director: If I remember correctly, when Martin joined us his father wanted him to be a priest, but Martin would not hear of it. He considered himself too unworthy.

Superior: Is it agreed then? Shall we try to persuade Martin to make vows as a Dominican brother?

Novice Director: Definitely.

Assistant: Of course.

Prayer Service

Song: "Whatsoever You Do," "This Is My Commandment," or "Service"

Leader: St. Martin de Porres spent his life doing good for others. He carried out the works of mercy Christ expects his followers to practice. These works help others in body and soul. They are mentioned in Jesus' parable about who would enter the kingdom.

Reading: Matthew 25:31–40 (The merciful will be rewarded on Judgment Day.)

Leader: Not only did St. Martin make others happy by his life of good deeds, this way of living also brought him great joy and peace. Let us pray to be like St. Martin who was like Jesus.

All: (The sentences may be sung to the melody of "Kum Ba Yah.")

When someone's hungry, Lord, let us help.

When someone's thirsty, Lord, let us help.

When someone needs clothes, Lord, let us help.

When someone's sick, Lord, let us help.

When someone's homeless, Lord, let us help.

When someone's lost, Lord, let us help.

When someone's frightened, Lord, let us help.

When someone's sad, Lord, let us help.

When someone's hurting, Lord, let us help

When someone's confused, Lord, let us help.

When someone needs a friend, Lord, let us help.

When someone needs prayers, Lord, let us help.

St. Martin: Brother Broom

Fill in the missing words. Then read the poem aloud.

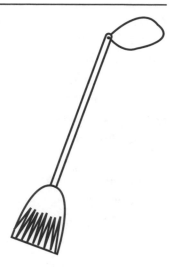

St. Martin de Porres was a saint through and through;
He came from the city of _____, Peru.

His father was Spanish, his mother was black;
Mr. Porres first left them, then later came back.

Though Martin, his mom, and his sister were poor,
He gave away money en route to the store.

A barber and _____ he soon trained to be;
The poor of the town he took care of for _____.

A prayerful young man, Martin answered God's call
To be a lay helper and give God his all.

He cleaned, swept, and prayed as a Dominican,
And cut hair and nursed about three hundred _____.

His powers of healing and unusual prayer
Showed Martin was holy beyond compare.

He cared for sick people and _____, too;
His sister Joan's house he turned into a zoo!

When cloth had been ruined by _____ without doubt,
He promised to feed them if they would move out.

By nine years St. Martin was finally a _____
Whose vows bound him fully to God and no other.

St. Martin lived poorly while serving the _____;
He taught, fed, and nursed them and then did much more.

With funds begged from friends he was able to build
An orphanage—home and school—that soon was filled.

He gave poor girls the money they needed to _____;
His fame spread beyond his own monastery.

Patron of _____ is the title he bears,
And Martin's still known as a person who cares.

Be Nice to Mice and Other Creatures

In each of the mice below write a way to be kind to God's creatures.

St. Lucy: Lady of Light

Died 304

For years families in Sweden have celebrated the feast of St. Lucy in a special way. For breakfast the oldest daughter dresses in white with a red sash around her waist. She wears a crown of evergreen branches with lighted candles. Then she serves the rest of the family coffee and Lucy buns. These are yellow sweet rolls in the shape of an S with spiraled ends. Who is this St. Lucy who has inspired such a ceremony?

A Short but Holy Life

During the late third century the church was being persecuted. The Roman emperors condemned Christians to death. At this time Lucy, a Christian girl, lived in the town of Sicily in Italy. Lucy loved Jesus so much that she wanted to live totally for him. She decided she would not marry. This was an unusual decision because in those days, women were expected to marry. Lucy's mother, Eutychia, did not understand her daughter. She encouraged Lucy to marry a man who wanted her for his bride. This man did not even believe in Christ. Lucy, who thought of herself as the bride of Christ alone, rejected the man's offer.

According to a story, Eutychia became very sick. Lucy persuaded her to make a pilgrimage, a holy journey, to the tomb of St. Agatha to pray for her recovery. St. Agatha, too, had been an unmarried Christian woman from Sicily. She had been killed for the faith about fifty years earlier. It is said that as Lucy and Eutychia prayed at her tomb, St. Agatha appeared to Lucy. She foretold that the people of the city of Syracuse would one day honor Lucy because she had kept her heart for Christ. Eutychia was cured and began to see Lucy's point of view. In fact, when Lucy wanted to distribute her fortune to the poor, her mother helped her.

Lucy's life of goodness and love was cut short, however, about the year 304, when she was around twelve years old. Supposedly, a young man who wanted to marry Lucy was insulted when she refused him. He reported to the government that she was a Christian.

Lucy was arrested and brought before the governor. With dignity and grace she answered questions. She explained, "You obey the emperor's laws; I obey God's laws. You try to please an earthly ruler; I try to please God." She did not deny her faith, not even when she was threatened. The governor was angry that this mere girl defied him. He ordered that she be taken to a house where prostitutes lived.

Guards grabbed hold of Lucy and tried to take her away, but they couldn't budge her! She had suddenly become very heavy. It is said that oxen were even brought in and fastened to Lucy with ropes in an attempt to pull her out. But still Lucy could not be moved.

Instead of being awed by these happenings, the governor just became angrier. He ordered that Lucy be burned to death. When a fire was set, again he was frustrated. The flames did not hurt her. Lucy in the meantime was praying and speaking to the people. Finally, a soldier killed her with his sword.

St. Lucy reminds us of Jesus' parable about the ten bridesmaids who were waiting for the bridegroom. Five of them ran out of oil and missed the wedding, but five of them were wise and had taken enough oil. They were on time for the wedding. Like the wise bridesmaids, Lucy had her lamp lit when the bridegroom came. In other words, although she died at such a young age, she had enough faith and good works to enter into the wedding feast of heaven.

Lady of the Light

The early Christians honored Lucy as a saint because she was martyred. Today her name, with St. Agatha's, is included in one of the Eucharistic Prayers at Mass. She is the patron of eyes. The reason is unknown. Perhaps it is because the name "Lucy" means light, and light enables us to see. Perhaps it is because Lucy's own eyes were harmed once and then healed, as some legends say.

According to another legend, once when the people in Lucy's country were starving, she prayed with them. As they prayed, a ship loaded with wheat sailed into their harbor and everyone had plenty to eat.

Lucy's feast day falls in Advent, the time when we are waiting for Jesus, who is the light of the world. The meteors, or falling stars, in the mornings and evenings of December are called Lucy stars.

Pictures and statues of Lucy usually show her with fire, a sword, or a palm branch, which is a symbol of the victory a martyr has won. Sometimes she is shown holding a plate with eyes on it!

St. Lucy demonstrates that you don't have to be old to be a saint. Young people can be saints too. All it takes is a great love of Jesus.

What Do You Think?

- How did Lucy have the courage to die for her faith?
- Lucy prayed to Agatha for help. Who are some special saints you can pray to in times of need?
- When would Lucy be a good person to pray to?
- How do some people today live totally for Jesus?
- What can you do to make your faith stronger?
- How can someone your age be holy?

Things to Do

1. Write a prayer thanking God for the gift of sight.
2. Jesus is the light of the world. Think of some situations where people need this light. Draw a picture of one such situation.
3. With a classmate, act out an interview of Eutychia about her daughter.
4. Find out about a group of martyrs, such as the Korean martyrs, the Vietnamese martyrs, the Japanese martyrs, the Ugandan martyrs, the North American martyrs, or the English martyrs. Write a report on one group.
5. Devise a way that you can contribute something to the poor.
6. Make a clay lamp or candle to remind you to keep your light alive.
7. Resolve to grow in faith by learning more about your Catholic faith.

8. Celebrate St. Lucy's feast day by eating cinnamon buns or Lucy buns. Ask an older person to help you follow this recipe for Lucy buns:

2 packages of dry yeast
1/2 cup warm water
1 cup warm milk
1 1/2 teaspoons salt
1/4 cup honey
1/2 cup butter
1 teaspoon ground cardamom
2 eggs
6-7 cups unbleached white flour
1 pinch of saffron or drop of yellow food coloring
1 egg white
raisins

Combine the yeast and water. In another bowl combine milk, honey, spices, and salt, and then add butter, eggs, and the yeast mixture. Beat in enough flour to make a stiff dough. Put the dough onto a lightly floured surface and knead it until smooth (about 10 minutes). Place it in a greased bowl, cover lightly, and allow it to rise for an hour. Knead the dough for 3 minutes. Return it to the bowl, cover it, and let it rise for 45 minutes. Punch it down, and knead it for 3 more minutes. Cover the dough and let it rest for 15 minutes. Divide the dough into 24 pieces and roll each into a foot-long rope. Form an *S* shape with the ropes on a greased baking sheet. Coil each end of the *S* until it looks like a double snail shell. Put raisins in the eye of each coil. Brush the buns with egg white and bake at 350° for 15 to 20 minutes. They will brown on top. Serve warm.

Craft: Star Mobile

Make a star mobile. Trace and cut out three or four stars from aluminum foil. Cut colored paper into three or four different shapes. On each one write a truth of our faith. Look in the Apostles' Creed for ideas. Punch holes in the stars and other shapes. String yarn or thread through them and tie them to a hanger. Put the mobile where it will remind you of the light of faith.

A Playlet: A Star from Sicily

Characters: Eutychia, Stella

(Eutychia is standing. Stella enters.)

Stella: Eutychia, my sympathy on the death of your daughter. I came as soon as I heard.

Eutychia: Thank you, Stella. How kind of you. Yes, my little Lucy is gone. She was too good for this world. We named her Lucy, which means light, and she was like a bright light in our house. I will miss her kindness and her laughter.

Stella: If it's any consolation to you, she was splendid in her death—so noble. A friend of mine was present. He said no matter how the official tried to turn her away from Christ, Lucy stood firm.

Eutychia: She would. She was always strong. Sometimes my husband and I considered her stubborn. When we wanted her to marry, she held out against us and insisted she belonged to Christ.

Stella: I remember. It wasn't until she took you to St. Agatha's shrine and you were healed from your illness that you let her be.

Eutychia: I didn't just let her be; she convinced me to help her. Together we distributed her inheritance to the poor. Lucy did extraordinary things for God.

Stella: And God did extraordinary things for her. When the guards tried to take her away, those big men weren't able to move that slip of a girl. My friend told me that they brought in oxen. Even they could not drag her out.

Eutychia: Yes, but in the end they killed her.

Stella: Right, but she still lives. We know that she is with Christ now and sees him face to face. How happy she must be, and how proud you can be of your daughter.

Eutychia: Father Stephen told me that Lucy is still a light. Now she is like a bright star shining in heaven for all eternity.

Stella: What a beautiful thing to say! And how true. Lucy leads the way for the rest of us, the way to eternal life. Take heart, good friend. We will soon see Lucy again.

Eutychia: But first I must be able to forgive the young man who reported her to the authorities as a Christian. He was angry that she wouldn't marry him. I'm praying to Lucy to soften my heart towards him. I'm sure she forgave him.

Stella: No doubt she did. That girl was a saint!

Prayer Service

Song: Hymn about light, such as "This Little Light of Mine," "We Are the Light of the World," "Light of the World," "Before the Sun Burned Bright," or "Like a Sunflower"

Leader: St. Lucy let the light of faith shine in her. Her love for God and her good works were plain for all to see. People who had no faith tried to put out her light. But because they took away her life on earth, Lucy's light has burned brightly down through almost eighteen centuries.

Reader: Matthew 5:14–16 (Be like a city on a mountain.)

Leader: Let us pray to have strong faith like Lucy's. The response is "Christ, be our light."

That you may be the center of our life, we pray…

That we may grow in understanding your teachings, we pray…

That we may look on our faith as something very precious, we pray…

That we may value ourselves as good people made and loved by God, we pray…

That we may see you in every person, we pray…

That we may regard the poor and needy as our brothers and sisters, we pray…

That we may avoid the darkness of sin, we pray…

That we may share the light of faith with others, we pray…

A Martyr's Crown

Design a crown for St. Lucy in the box below. Choose symbols and colors that represent her.

The Light of Faith

Use the code to discover the faith statement that guided Lucy's life.

✚	■	◯	◳	◆	▢	●	✖	♣	✳	✦	⊘	☆	▲
A	D	E	F	G	I	J	L	N	O	R	S	U	V

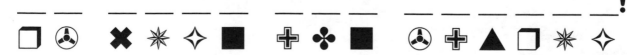

Answers:

Page 8 (St. Elizabeth)

First community of women, first parochial school, first hospital, first orphanage, first native-born saint to be canonized

Page 14 (St. Peter)

Fishing For Words

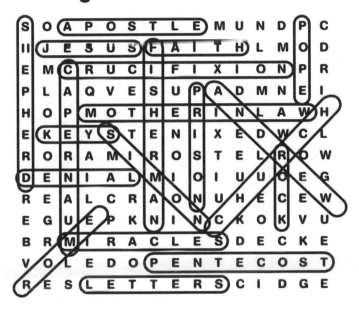

Page 20 (St. Joseph)

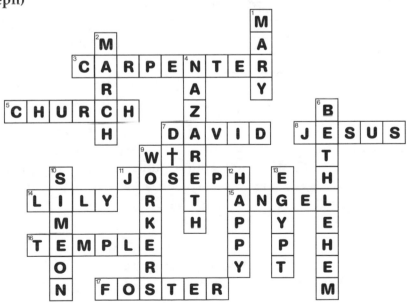

Page 25 (St. Catherine)

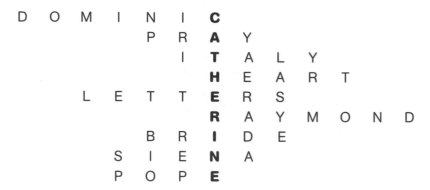

```
D O M I N I C
          P R A Y
          I   T A L Y
          I   H E A R T
L E T T E R S
          B R I D E
S I E N A
P O P E
```

Page 31 (St. Isidore)

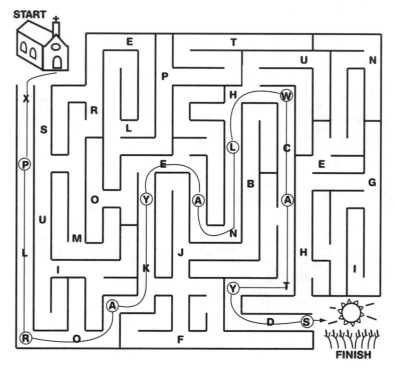

Message: Pray always.

Page 40 (St. Ignatius)

ant(s), as, at, gain, gait, gas, gin, gist, gnat(s), gnu(s), gun(s), gust, in, is, it, nag(s), nit(s), nut(s), sag, saint, sang, sat, satin, sign, sin, sing, sit, snag, snit, snug, stag, stain, sting, stun, suing, suit, sun, sung, tag(s), tan(s), tang, tin, us

Page 45 (St. Clare)

These areas should be shaded to reveal a monstrance:

Agnes, Assisi, August, begging, Blessed Sacrament, Francis, penance, Poor Clares, prayer, San Damiano, Saracens, sickness, television

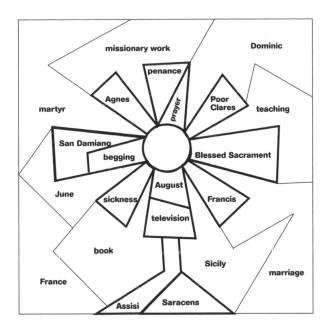

Page 50 (St. Vincent)

For what you have done to the least of these you have done to me.

Pages 56–57 (St. Francis)

My God and my all.

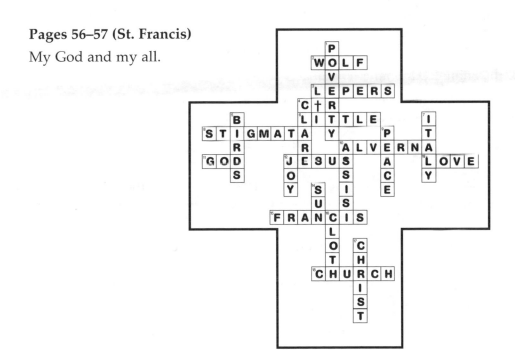

Page 62 (St. Martin)

Lima, doctor, free, men, animals, mice, brother, poor, marry, social justice

Page 68 (St. Lucy)

Jesus, Son of God, is Lord and Savior!

Resources

Videos

Saints for All Seasons. 8 videos. (Twenty-Third Publications, PO Box 180, Mystic, CT, 06355, 1-800-321-0411)

Saints' Gallery series. 3 videos. Videos with Values.

Books

Foley, Leonard, O.F.M., ed. *Saint of the Day* (2 volumes). Cincinnati: St. Anthony Messenger Press, 1990.

Langdon, Larry. *Children Celebrate: 39 Plays for Feasts.* Cincinnati: St. Anthony Messenger Press, 1993.

Lodi, Enzo. *Saints of the Roman Calendar.* Staten Island, NY: Alba House, 1992.

McGinley, Phyllis. *Saint-Watching.* New York: Doubleday, 1974.

Nevins, Albert J. *A Saint for Your Name (Boys)* and *A Saint for Your Name (Girls).* Huntington, IN: Our Sunday Visitor, 1980.

Odell, Catherine, and Margaret Savitskas. *Saints in Action.* Mission Hills, CA: Benziger, 1997.

Sisters of Notre Dame. *Saints and Feast Days: Lives of the Saints: With a Calendar and Ways to Celebrate.* Chicago: Loyola Press, 1985.

Walsh, Michael, ed. *Butler's Lives of the Saints,* concise edition. New York: HarperCollins, 1991.

Vision books (Lives of the Saints). San Francisco: Ignatius Press.

Woodward, Kenneth L. *Making Saints: How the Catholic Church Determines Who Becomes a Saint, Who Doesn't, and Why.* New York: Simon & Schuster, 1990.

Multimedia

Saints Kit. (Loyola Press, 3441 N. Ashland Ave., Chicago, IL 60657; 1-800-621-1008) This is a set of 189 cards (6 1/2" x 9"), one for each saint of the Roman Calendar with a picture, a biography, and activities.

Holy Trader Cards. (Holy Traders, PO Box 1794, Ft. Collins, CO 80522; 1-800-242-8467) These are baseball card-size pictures of the saints with an explanation.

Bridge-Building Images. (Bridge Building, PO Box 1048, Burlington, VT 05402; 1-802-864-8346) These present the saints in the style of the eastern church.

Saints Cards. (Silver Burdett Ginn, Customer Service Center, 4350 Equity Drive, PO Box 2649, Columbus, OH 43216; 1-800-848-9500) These are colorful cards for every grade (6 saints per grade, 30 duplicate cards for each saint to distribute to your class), each including a prayer.

Music

The suggested songs for the prayer services can be found in parish hymnals, such as *Breaking Bread* and *Glory and Praise* (Oregon Catholic Press), *Worship, Gather,* and *Lead Me, Guide Me* (GIA Publications), and *We Celebrate* and *People's Mass Book* (World Library Publications).

Praying with the Saints
30 Classroom Services for Children
Gwen Costello

Catechists and students (grades 3 to 6) will enjoy using these 30 creative prayer services and activities, each of which focuses on an aspect of a saint's life that children can imitate. Each service begins with a brief introduction, a mini-biography of the saint, followed by ideas for prayer, an action response, and an optional activity.

112 pp, $12.95 (order J-30)

Mystics & Martyrs, Healers & Hermits, Soldiers & Seekers...
Stories of Saints through the Centuries
Anne Neuberger

Share with your students (grades 3 to 6) the fascinating story of saints who lived during the 20 centuries of Christianity, with its lights and shadows, its varied situations, problems, and personalities. Included are historical and cultural background information and activities that help the students connect the saints' examples to their own lives.

120 pp, $12.95 (order J-31)

Saints for Our Time
Ed Ransom

Presents each saint as a real person, with the same problems, hopes, fears, and dreams as the reader. There are saints for every person and personality, each with a different set of qualities, talents, weaknesses, and attributes. Written in response to the needs of catechumens and RCIA candidates, this volume is recommended reading for every catechist, teacher, student.

304 pp, $14.95 (order B-38)

Book of Saints
Michael Walsh

Here is a saint for each week of the year, some well-known, and some who deserve to be so. Each saint's biography opens with an illuminated capital that depicts a scene or notable quality identified with that saint. These saints can serve to renew our own commitment to faith, prayer, and loving service.

160 pp, $9.95 (order M-20)

Saints Alive
Stories and Activities for Young Children
Gayle Schreiber

Here is a delightful book of short stories illustrating the lives of 30 saints for children in grades pre-K through three. Each story focuses on a positive aspect of the saint's life, offers a prayer to that saint, and includes an activity page.

72 pp, $9.95 (order M-68)

Available at religious bookstores or from:

TWENTY-THIRD PUBLICATIONS

P.O. BOX 180 • 185 WILLOW ST. • MYSTIC, CT 06355 • 1-860-536-2611 • 1-800-321-0411 • FAX 1-800-572-0788

Call for a free catalog